# LOLLIPOPS OF DUST

First edition
published in 2011 by

Woodfield Publishing Ltd
Bognor Regis PO21 5EL England
www.woodfieldpublishing.co.uk

© Susan Read-Lobo, 2011

ISBN 1-84683-110-5

Printed and bound in England

Cover design by Mike Rowland

# Lollipops of Dust

*Memories of an African Childhood 1955-66*

Susan Read-Lobo

Woodfield

## Woodfield Publishing Ltd

Bognor Regis ~ West Sussex ~ England ~ PO21 5EL
**tel** 01243 821234 ~ **e/m** info@woodfieldpublishing.co.uk

*Interesting and informative books on a variety of subjects*

For full details of all our published titles, visit our website at
**www.woodfieldpublishing.co.uk**

*To the men in my life: Carlos my husband, my sons
Ivan and Xavier, my brother and my father.*

*Through me, this history is yours too.*

*I also dedicate this story to all those
who played a part in that history.*

*Thank you, you are not forgotten.*

*The Kalahari was ugly and it was beautiful, it was noisy and it was silent. It was empty and it was seething. As the Bushman said, "you have to know how to listen and know how to see."*

# ~ CONTENTS ~

# The Author

Susan Greta Read-Lobo was born in Guildford, Surrey in 1953. Just after she was born, her parents moved to London, where she lived until the age of two and a half, when she was taken to Africa. This book tells the story of the rest of her life until the present. She lives with her Spanish husband in Spain. She has two grown up sons. Susan has published a book of poetry entitled *Africa my Africa* and has won several poetry and short story competitions on local radio stations in the past.

*Susan Read-Lobo.*

# Acknowledgements

I would like to thank my wonderful Carlos for his patience while I wrote this book and also to my son Xavier in compiling the work, because his computer knowledge is better than mine and without his help I couldn't have done it.

I thank Carlos, Ivan and Xavier for their ears, which they have allowed me to bend over the years with my tales of lost worlds that today are invisible.

Thank you to Nicholas and all the Woodfield Publishing team for their kind help and advice, which makes a journey like this a pleasure rather than a pain.

# *Preface*

Botswana has never left my heart and mind, even after all these years. I had always thought that my memories should be put down on paper but life got in the way and I never got around to it. On reaching a time of life when one takes stock of what one has done with the years, together with a period of ill health, I decided to try to get my thoughts in some sort of order.

As I began to jot down memories, I realised that the fine details of one's life are so easy to mislay and that it would be such a pity to lose that very special time in history. This is a book of small vignettes to depict everyday life in the bush, at times in the middle of nowhere. In the course of writing, I sometimes had to stop because it became so emotional.

In later life, the knowledge that I was a white child from a colonial family has not been easy for me. I came to reassess certain situations I encountered as a child, the implications of which I was not aware at the time. We children we were cared for by maids, sent to boarding schools in far flung places from the age of 6, often while our parents slowly drank themselves into oblivion. On the positive side, we were left to wander around the bush and came to know Africa and its wild creatures and secret places in a way that nobody today could imagine. Not even our parents knew the Africa that we children knew. We lived outdoors in the sunshine, running free and wild. The problem came when the colonial era ended and we had to go back to the UK and adapt. Viewed as a whole, it was a bitter/sweet experience, hence the title of this book.

# *Introduction*

This book is a pot-pourri of anecdotes from the fading memory of a middle aged woman, going back in time through the eyes of the child she was, many moons ago, to the good/bad old days of life in colonial Africa, Botswana to be precise, formerly Bechuanaland Protectorate, or "the old B.P.", as it was affectionately known to one and all. I say good/bad days because, as with anything in life, there were pros and cons living in the colonies and I have seen many ex-colonial children become victims of the life their parents took them to. Heavy drinking, affairs and abuse were commonplace and for the kids, boarding schools were a must, with no educational facilities being available in far flung villages. Once the children reached a certain age, usually at six or even younger, if the parents wanted to get on with the serious business of hard partying without the hindrance of small children in the way, clamouring for attention, they would be packed off to school.

But that is another story and not what I want to tell you about in this book. I want to leave a legacy for my own children, a history of what being a little white girl child in Africa in the 1950s was like. A little girl who had no say in the matter of moving from England with its grey skies and soft green meadows, to a continent that was so alien, so harsh in light and heat, but so important in shaping the future of this little person.

This is an amble through my fading memories. The facts are all true, but the exact dates and details have drifted like the African winds that blow over the Kalahari – a place that I loved – and have no doubt mingled with that ancient dust. My mother is no longer here to corroborate and my dear father's memory goes back no further than what he had for breakfast, if he's lucky, bless him. So my dear readers, if you would like a peek into the past, into an Africa that didn't belong to us but which we took as ours, to do with what we wanted, I invite you to amble with me along this path, to keep me company on my journey back into childhood.

I must stress that this is not a novel, nor a diary, just a walk back into time with one anecdote following another. I have divided it up into the villages where we lived at the time of my tales in each place.

I have changed the names of people in the book to protect their privacy and that of their families. Most of the people I talk about I haven't seen for fifty years or so and many are not living anymore.

# 1.   My Background

My father Fearon came from a very aristocratic family and I say aristocratic as an attitude rather than a titled way. His father Robert, my grandpa, ran a rubber plantation in Ceylon, now Sri Lanka and my grandma Helen, was a nurse. They met on the ship going out to Ceylon and my father was born out there. My poor Dad had a rather chequered childhood and was sent to various boarding schools in England and South Africa. Only the best for this lonely little boy. He finished his education in Oxford and became a paratrooper in the army, doing a stint in Palestine.

My mother Evelyn was quite the opposite to my father in that she came from a humble coal mining village in the South of Wales. She was the younger of two girls. Her father Jim was a coal miner during the week and a lay preacher on Sundays, making my mother and her sister Maude dress up in their Sunday best to go to chapel three times on Sundays, turning my mother into a lifelong atheist and a strong determination to leave the beautiful but suffocating valleys as soon as she was old enough. My Grandma Myra was a knuckle-sore little lady who kept the home fires burning, the hearth polished, her two little girls scrubbed clean till they bled, because cleanliness was next to Godliness and being poor was no excuse for grime, not even the coal dust that lay on every surface in that valley. My grandpa was once trapped in the mine and there was always a shortage of money, so they didn't have an easy time of it at all. My mother decided to go away to study nursing when she was eighteen and after her training in Cardiff, she got a job in Oxford, where she met and became engaged to a pianist. This young man was pallid, languid and sad, with long, soft, white, fingers. While at a university party, she met my father, who was a very different personality she was used to. He was short, balding, extremely funny, highly intelligent, had travelled the world and to top it all, he rode a motor bike with a side- car. My father fell in love with my mother at first sight. Her sparkling blue eyes, ruby red lips, blonde hair and curvy figure decided it for him, so they became a couple and married a year later.

When they first married they lived in Guildford where I was born shortly afterwards and then moved to the centre of London. Dad worked for a big petroleum company and Mum washed nappies and hung them out under grey skies to never dry. They had a lot of bohemian friends from the theatre, film, the queen's guards and the literary and political world, so there were a lot of crazy parties, but they were restless and they wanted the sun.

Dad joined the colonial service and was offered a post in Bechuanaland Protectorate (B.P), now Botswana, but I shall refer to it through the book as the BP. The pay wasn't great, as I was to learn as I grew up, but it was the adventure that my parents craved and it was sunny. They would be stationed in far off remote villages and would be given three months overseas leave every two years, which would be taken by mail ship from South Africa or Mozambique to England and would take approximately three weeks there and three weeks back, which left the rest of the time divided between Dad's parents in the Isle of Wight, in a huge mansion with rolling gardens and Mum's parents in Blaenavon in the South of Wales, in a tiny little semi with an outside privy and a big copper tub put in front of the fire to bath in.

Before leaving London my parents rushed me around in a pushchair to see all the sights, as if this frantic glut of culture would seep into my small brain and serve as some sort of protection against what we were facing in deepest darkest Africa.

The friends and grandparents were said farewell to, amongst the many remarks of, "why Africa?" and, "you won't like it, you'll be home before you know it."

Now this is where my real story begins.

# 2.　Africa Here We Come

I was only two and a half when we embarked on our adventure. We didn't take much with us, as the government were to supply us with a fully furnished house in every place where we were to reside, so we just took clothes. These clothes were bought from a list supplied to us, recommending garments suitable for the tropics, which today would make most people smile. Ladies had to have cocktail wear and white cotton gloves and hats for garden parties. There was an evening-wear list and a day-wear list, together with special- occasion wear list, one for ladies and one for gentlemen. Children were advised to be covered up from the sun at all times. We were given another list of all medicines needed against all sorts of horrible tropical diseases and a further list of what to do and not do while out there – how to treat the natives and what to beware of, both from the natives, wild animals and creepy crawlies. Quite a daunting experience we were undertaking and thankfully I wasn't aware of anything else but the upheaval. I just floated along with my excited parents, without being aware of what was in store for us. Before leaving, we had to have all the necessary inoculations against even more nasties and the side effects were nasty in themselves, but we survived. We also had to start taking quinine before leaving, for malaria and it turned us an interesting shade of yellow that stayed with us until we left Africa ten years later. It was called Sunday-Sunday *muti. Muti* was the African term for all medicines and we had to take a pill every Sunday.

I remember being all dressed up and holding Mummy and Daddy's hands, one on each side of me as we walked up the gangplank of this beautiful lilac and white Union Castle ship, with the smoking red and black funnel. The captain was at the top waiting to meet us, all dressed in his navy uniform, which was his winter outfit, later to be changed for a white uniform when we entered warmer climes. Our cabin was lovely, rather like a dolls house to my mind at that age. The nursery was fun and I made a lot of friends. The food was lovely, served by friendly waiters on lovely china.

Leaving port, and indeed any port from then on, was an emotional event with everyone on board and the people on the quayside all waving hankies, the band playing and the flags and streamers flying was all so colourful and jolly. There were fancy dress parties for the children, costume balls for the adults, all sorts of sports, parties, cinema and events, the best being the crossing of the equator, when King Neptune and his briny men would come on board from their salty depths, to make us go through a ceremony that would guarantee our safety on his seas and would ensure us of a certificate to prove we had actually done it. It was such fun. As the years went by, I accumulated ten of these certificates but sadly today, with all my traveling, I don't have any left, they seem to have disappeared with time and miles, like so many accumulated items that one collects on the path of life. I had a couple of birthdays on board, through the years that I travelled on Union Castle ships and they were special too, because the captain would invite me to his cabin and give me a present and then I would be given a party in the dining room.

At all the fancy dress parties my mother dressed me up as Lady Greensleeves, sewing a costume of different green crepe leaves that covered me from head to toe and I always won first prize with that outfit, so something must have worked its magic and I have always loved that tune which was played as I entered the ballroom dressed as Lady Greensleeves.

In the run up to the fancy dress parties, both adult and children's, the shop on board did a roaring trade in crepe paper, glue, funny hats and sewing equipment. All the mums would sit huddled on the deck, in the various lounges, around the pool and in their cabins, sewing and gluing secret outfits that were only to be seen in their entirety on the big night.

There was an air of festivity on the ship. I had the run of the ship, but there were always two places I loved the most. One was the silent, musty, dusty library, where very old tomes sat side by side on dark mahogany shelves, willing to tell their stories to anyone who dared take them gently down and dip into them. This sacred place was never crowded but there were always a few very old people, all with spectacles perched on the end of their noses, old gents noses sprouting hairs in odd places that quivered when they snored and old ladies noses, powdered in dusty rose face-powder, usually Rubenstein or Elizabeth Arden, forming thick tracks in the deep lines of their aged faces.

I loved observing these living history books, wondering where they had all come from and where they were all going to, both on this ship and in their dreams, as they quietly nodded off over these dusty tomes, lulled by the gentle swell of the ocean. I was just as fascinated by the old books as I was by the old people there; I felt that they were part of the ship.

The other place I loved was the lounge. I used to try to get away from my parents at three o clock because it was teatime, I would go into this magical elegant lounge with beautiful sea views from every angle and I would sit myself down in an elegant chintz armchair. The waiter in white gloves would come up and ask me what I wanted by saying, "and what can I get you today madam?", with a secret smile on his lips, hiding the fact that he was humouring a little girl, who took her role very seriously indeed. I would order tea which would come in a beautiful silver teapot and he would pour it for me into a rose patterned cup sitting daintily on a matching saucer and would ask, "one lump or two?" and with the engraved tongs, plop the sugar cubes into my tea. Then he would bring a plate of dainty triangle sandwiches with the crust cut off and fillings of salmon, egg and cress, or cucumber, followed with a four-tiered silver platter bearing all sorts of iced delicacies. I would cock my little finger pretending to be the Lady of the Manor and then wade into everything that was offered to me.

On the winter crossings, we were given beef tea on deck and in summer, ice cream. There would be tea and biscuits in bed before breakfast and the menus were spectacular and it was no wonder that I became a real little barrel. At almost three, I already knew that I appreciated the good things in life, a real little madam. I can still smell the corridors of the ship, a smell not repeated anywhere else I have ever been.

We stopped at lots of exotic ports, islands and countries through the years too, which was an education in itself for a growing child. I am just glossing over the voyages as a whole, because they don't make ships like that anymore and there are many people who served in the colonies who remember the Union Castle line as something very special. They took so many folk to and from Africa and they looked after us like royalty. I doubt whether one could get a cruise like that today, with the exception of the *Queen Mary* maybe. Nevertheless, my first voyage out to Africa comes in flashes, but as I got older and went on overseas leave with my parents, I began to enjoy and appreciate all these trips and remember many details.

When we finally got to Cape Town we were given a car and had to drive up through South Africa into the B.P. to our first station – Lobatsi. We arrived at night, hot and tired, so we went to a small local hotel, where we fell into a deep sleep. The next day we set out to explore and what a shock. Mum cried her eyes out because it was so dry and dusty; a grey place covered by a blanket of grey dust. The sun beat down on this grey dust and the only things that moved were the flies. This was our new home; welcome to Africa!

From here on, I shall recall little incidents, anecdotes, short tales, pearls or whatever you like to call them, dipping in and out of past memories. I was a lonely little girl living in lonely places, left mostly to myself while the grownups got on with the business of running the lives of the natives and living the colonial life of sundowners and parties. The natives looked after us probably better that we looked after them. They washed, ironed, cleaned, scrubbed, cooked, washed up, gardened and looked after the white children in their care, of which I was one and am eternally grateful, because without them I would have been even lonelier that I was. So I am asking you to be my friend and take my hand and follow me into the past and pretend that you are a little child with me, because all those adventures many years ago would have been so much more fun if I could have shared them with a friend.

# 3.     Lobatsi and the House

That first morning we were taken to our new home, a low house with a *stoep* running around it, covered with mosquito mesh. The rooms were big and airy with old furniture that didn't match. I do not remember how my mother felt on seeing this, but it didn't really affect me in any way. I was more interested in the garden because coming from a flat in the centre of London, a garden was a novelty. It was a big garden with all sorts of shrubs and plants that I cannot remember the names of but I do remember the Syringa tree in the middle of a yellow, dried-out, scrubby lawn. This tree was the only shade around and against all odds, it flowered beautiful lilac blossoms that drifted down on top of you when you sat underneath it. This tree was to be my play place, my territory. At the back of the house were the servants' quarters, as yet without servants, but that was soon to change, because bush telephone was soon at work among the neighbourhood maids, that there was a new master and madam in residence.

Our direct neighbour was a white doctor from South Africa and was a very nice man and a real help at times when we needed a doctor. My memories of this outpost are few because I was so young and hadn't really the ability to form ideas or opinions, but I mention this place because it is where we started out.

Our house was haunted. Now you may not believe in these things, nor did my parents, at least until they were forced into it by certain circumstances.

The furniture that came with the house was old, very dark, heavy and rather tatty, but in the bush these details didn't count for much. My mother went about making a home of this house the best she could. She and I would go for long walks into the scrubby bush surrounding the house, looking for long dry reeds, seeds, pods and leaves, that she would stick in a pot to make the place look more like home. Soon African grass mats and animal skins covered the red polished floors that were waxed every week and smelt of polish. Mum was very artistic with swathes of African cloth draped over old sofas and chairs, or hung over windows to block out the permanent white glare. At times, the curtains would be taken down, draped around my mother, secured with a big brooch and topped with a turban and a big pair of earrings and she was ready for another cocktail party. The curtains always went up again afterwards. Such was life in the bush, where there were no shops selling soft furnishings or high fashion, so we made do.

Getting back to the haunted house, at night we would hear furniture being scraped across the floor and on getting up, found all the furniture in the house changed position. At first, we thought that someone had got into the house, but nothing had been taken. It got so that even during the day pieces would elevate off the floor and float about in front of us. There was nothing we could do to stop it and eventually we just accepted it as something we had to live with, although it did mean more work for Mum putting everything back in its place.

My mother found the heat draining and decided to employ some servants for the housework, as everyone had advised her to do. She had never had servants before and was rather unsure as to whether she wanted anyone around the house, but it was all part of the colonial way of life. Word soon got around that there were two jobs going for grabs. One only had to think these things, it seemed, and the bush crackled with a silent energy that attracted a queue of people outside the kitchen door. Mum interviewed a lot of young girls that were virtually children and most of them didn't speak English, which was no good at all. After almost giving up hope, one morning an older woman came knocking at the door. She had a colourful *doek* (head scarf) on her head and deep tribal cuts on both cheeks, which looked quite frightening, but besides speaking her own language Setswana, she spoke perfect English, as well as

Afrikaans and a couple of other African tongues including the Bushmen's 'click' language. Agnes or Aggie, as she liked to be called, lived in the nearby village, in a mud hut with her eight children of various ages and by various men, who had all left her to bring up her children on her own, with the help of surrounding extended family members. She was also a staunch Roman Catholic and believed in a fierce God and a hell of fire and brimstone.

She was hired on the spot as nanny, cook, cleaner, to do the washing (without washing machine), the ironing (with heavy irons heated up on a permanently lit wood stove), serve at table, deliver tea in bed to the masters in the morning before breakfast, make bread (fresh for the day before breakfast), etc. In fact, Aggie took over our home and our lives and practically became the madam of the mansion. I loved her more than anyone in the world and she loved me back, fiercely.

The day she started work was quite exciting for us, not having had a servant before and Mum was all of a twitter, but she needn't have been because the minute Aggie walked through the door with the confidence only she possessed, there was a calm over the whole house. She set to work like a whirlwind and soon the whole place smelt of polish, soap, fresh-cut flowers (which she changed every day), lemons (which she picked from the tree in the garden) and fresh-baked bread and cakes, which she made for "my little Suzie" (me).

I will always remember her first day at work; we were sitting on the old, chipped kitchen step overlooking the back yard. It was a very hot and windy day with squalls of dust rising up in little whirlwind formations, lifting all the grey dust and rubbish with it and depositing it everywhere, both in and out of the house, in eyes and mouth, everywhere. Aggie was sipping her strong *rooibos* tea, sweetened with a good dollop of condensed milk, her eyes narrowed to prevent the dust and she looked ancient to me, although we never knew her age and she didn't either. I was watching her closely. She fascinated me because I had never had contact with anyone like her before and I stuck to her side constantly. She put her hand in the pocket of her pink maid's uniform, brought out a lollipop and handed it to me saying, "I bring you a present." I had never seen a lollipop like this before; it was huge and bright pink, a gobstopper on a stick. I could barely get it into my mouth, much to the amusement of Aggie. I don't know where it came from because it didn't have a wrapper on it and it had a bit of grey fluff stuck to it from the bottom of Aggie's pocket, but it didn't matter. It didn't matter either that it was cloyingly sweet and sticky in the heat; it was the best present I had had for a long time. I think it was the fact that this woman, whom I found so intriguing, had given me something. The day being as it was, didn't help either, because every time I manoeuvred this huge lollipop out of my mouth, a gust of gritty grey dust would coat the pink orb entirely. Aggie said I should throw it away but there was no way that I was going to get rid of this treasure. It got grittier and grittier every time it came out of my mouth but I would pop it back in, grit and all. I told Aggie that it was a lollipop of dust and it was my favourite taste in all the world. My immune system was put to test from that day on and I became a strong, brown, little African white girl, as hard as nails, like the bush surrounding me, but always protected by my Aggie.

Mum also employed a 'garden boy', as they were called back then, even if they were fully-grown men. His name was Benson and he was very tall and very black, almost a blue/black, with sheen to his skin that made it look as though it was always wet. He had very white eyes and teeth and was very serious. Benson was nice but I didn't take to him as I did to Aggie. His job was to do the gardening as best he could in the heat and to polish the house floors with the thick red polish that, if you weren't careful, would stain everything. Benson wore a thick off-white shirt and big, matching drawstring shorts, rimmed with red binding, the outfit worn by all the boys in domestic service. On his feet he wore sandals made of old car tyres. He lived in the servants' quarters at the bottom of the yard because Aggie went home to the location at the end of the day. Sometimes she would stay and babysit for me when Mum and Dad went out for dinner or a function. Poor Benson wasn't in good health and had to take liver pills every day, usually after he had been on a bender on his weekend off. Servants came and servants went during our stay in Africa, some were good and some were not, but Aggie was always with us. Even when we went for our three months overseas leave every two years, she would know beforehand where we were going to be stationed and when we returned, she would be there waiting for us, to get our new home ship shape for us. She crossed the country in every direction, following us wherever we went, leaving her children in the care of family members. Sometimes she would send a message to her village to bring one of her children to stay with her for a while, which was fun for me to have someone to play with. When we left Lobatsi after two years' service there, she always lived in the servants quarters that we had in our yard and she always made her home so pretty and cosy. She ruled the roost and was in charge of every other servant working for us, giving orders and keeping everything running. When we finally left Bechuanaland, when it became Botswana, on September 30th 1966 and went back to England, Aggie retired, going back to her village in Lobatsi.

*My Invisible Friend Miriam*

While I was playing under my Syringa tree one hot drowsy afternoon, running in and out of the sprinkler, I was suddenly confronted with a little blonde girl of about my age. She had curly hair and a white dress on, which I thought odd, as it was so hot; I just had on a little pair of shorts. I asked her where she came from and she said "here" and when I asked her name, she told me it was "Miriam and would I mind playing with her?" I was delighted to have a little friend to play with and we chatted away. Every afternoon she appeared, always dressed the same and we always played just like all little girls have always played. One afternoon Mum looked out of the window and saw me chatting away, so she called me and asked whom I was talking to. I told her I was talking to my new friend Miriam and that she came every day to play, but Mum was perplexed because she couldn't see anyone with me. After this had gone on for a couple of weeks Mum decided to take me next door to see our neighbour the doctor. She told him that she was worried because I had an invisible friend and she thought that I was taking this normal childhood phase a little too far. The doctor took me to his examining room and questioned me, asking me all about my friend. He wanted to know what she looked like, what her name was, how old she was and some other questions about her clothes. Afterwards he went to see Mum and told her that there was an explanation to my friend. He knew the people who stayed in the house before we arrived there and they had a little girl called Miriam of the age I described. Miriam was killed by a snake under the same Syringa tree not long before we arrived and the family left the house after the accident. All this explains why our furniture was moved around so much, it was Miriam making her presence known and I continued to play with her until we left the house.

## Pets ~ My Best Friends

I was still too young for school and there were no nursery schools around, so I was pretty lonely and Mum and Dad decided to get me a couple of pets to keep me company, a cat and a dog. I remember the day we went to get my puppy from a family just wanting to find homes for these ugly little creatures. I say ugly because they were a mixture of every breed of dog available. When we arrived there were only two of the litter left, curled up in a wicker basket fast asleep. I was told that I could choose whichever I wanted so I promptly chose the ugliest, a little male with black curls and a little orange goatee beard. I called him Jason, which soon became Jaggers and then Jags. Jags became my shadow and followed me everywhere I went. Not long afterwards, we got a cat called Marmaduke, a huge ginger fellow, as soft as butter in that he would let me do anything to him. I would dress this poor cat up in tight swaddling, tie a doll's bonnet down over his little face and stick a pop- bottle of milk, with a teat attached, into his mouth while I pushed him around the yard singing lullabies, in temperatures of over a hundred. Poor Marmaduke didn't have a voice; he was born mute and couldn't meow at all, so he just had to take it all in silence.

Later, on another station we lived in, we had a cross between a Dalmatian and something else strange, called Tuli, after the Tuli Block, which was the area we lived in. By the time we got Tuli, Jags had died in a dogfight with a pit bull. He loved a good fight and it was the end of him eventually, after about six years with us. Apart from these two dogs and Marmaduke, we had numerous other animals during our ten years in the bush. Whenever there was an animal orphaned by hunters or wild animals, the rangers would bring us these vulnerable little creatures, usually in a state of shock, so that we could nurture them until they could be weaned back into the bush by the rangers themselves. We had numerous and a wide variety of buck, a couple of baby elephant, a few felines of different sorts, little lion cubs, cheetahs, a baby leopard and even a baby hippo at one stage. This little fellow wandered up to our garden from the river by himself. I don't think he was an orphan, I think he had just gone for a walk, leaving his worried Mum fretting in the reeds. He came into our garden, chomped up all our flowers and then left again, to, I suspect, go back to his Mum.

As a child growing up in the bush without much other company, this parade of animals was a great solace to me and as I spoke to them, they seemed to understand me and I them. The bird life was amazing too, so many varieties, colours, bird song and different nests. Dad was a great bird watcher; he and I would sometimes go out together with a pair of binoculars, a notebook and a copy of Robinson's bird book and he would make notes on all we saw and heard. But more often than not, he would escape on his own, leaving me behind because he thought I was too noisy to go along and would frighten the birds away. Mum being a nurse was a dab hand at fixing bird's broken wings. I know she said often enough that nursing people wasn't the same as nursing birds, but she had quite a high success rate. She would first dribble some brandy into the bird's beak, saying that it was good for shock in bird and human and then put their wing in a splint made of matchsticks. Many a bird flew off after a couple of weeks care. We had eagles, doves, owls and many little ones of various plumages.

All the houses that we lived in, as with every other house in the B.P., had a stoep that was meshed in to prevent mosquitoes, all manner of creepy crawlies and snakes from getting in. At least that was the idea, but every living creature on the African continent came into our home, wherever we were living. The geckoes used to come out at night and run along the mesh and have a feast on all sorts of insects attracted by the light. Our lighting was paraffin lamps and candles, as there was no electricity. No television, no radio, no light pollution, just bush sounds and stars.

Chameleons were also in abundance in our homes, they would appear from nowhere and saunter around the meshing, flicking their long sticky tongues out at anything passing their orbital eyes. We had great fun picking these creatures up and putting them onto colourful clothing and watching them change colour. In our gardens, we had a colourful array of butterflies and dragonflies of all the colours of the rainbow and watching them all dip in and out of the lawn sprinkler they resembled precious stones glistening in the water. We had frogs and toads, tortoises and porcupines and African millipedes in shiny black, virulent yellow and scarlet, also known as *songololos* and came from minute to enormous in size. There were lizards and beetles of all sizes and colours. There, all sorts of insects that could bite, sting you and even kill you, scorpions and snakes being among the most deadly.

I can remember Mum and Dad sitting in the garden one evening, having the eternal sundowner, when suddenly there was a swishing sound and down came these huge moths that looked like cleaning cloths. They perched on the glasses containing beer, put down a proboscis into the beer, sucked it up until the glasses were empty and then flew off. I have been petrified of moths ever since.

There are some beautiful trees in Southern Africa called *Mopane* trees, they have a shiny rounded butterfly shaped leaves in a bright green with a pinkish blush that fold in half in intense heat. In these trees there are usually *mopane worms* feeding off the leaves and they are a great delicacy in those parts. These worms are fat and a mixture of bright colours and a black tipped head and tail. Aggie taught me to nip off the bottom end and squeeze the brightly coloured innards out, which were then grilled in hot coals and eaten crispy, or they could be dried in the sun. I loved them, much to the disgust of my parents, who were beginning to wonder whether they had done the right thing by bringing me to this savage country. Another tasty treat was the flying ant. Usually these creatures would arrive in abundance once the rains had fallen and we would collect them in buckets, take off their wings and fry them or eat them raw. They tasted of peanut butter.

Snakes were the great fear of everyone in the B.P. because they were everywhere and got into the house and most of them were very poisonous. We had a snake serum kit at home but one had to act very quickly in the case of snakebite. One of my kittens, Chloe, was killed by a snake and it broke my heart. As a child, although I was aware of snakes everywhere, because it was such a major thing in everyday life, I wasn't afraid of them. I think I had the innocence of childhood and felt that if I didn't hurt them, then they wouldn't hurt me. I would actually catch them, bring them into my bed at night when nobody was looking, and then be more surprised in the morning that they were gone, instead of the fact that they hadn't bitten me. I guess I was lucky, but I like to think that I was a friend of the bush and its wild inhabitants; they were my only friends.

*Aggie's Mud Hut ~ With My Help*

One day Aggie came into the kitchen and asked my mother for a day off because she wanted to finish a hut she had been building with her family. The walls and the thatching were completed and now just the floor needed finishing. Mum said she could take the next day off to add to the following one, which was her day free anyway, giving her two days to complete her task. I asked if I could go with Aggie to help her with her hut but was told in no uncertain terms by Mum that I wasn't to be so ridiculous. That was no place for a little girl like me and I would just get in Aggie's way. I yelled, cried, screamed and had the tantrum to beat all tantrums until Aggie said that she would be willing to take me with her the next day and bring me back the same evening. Mum backed down and although she wasn't very happy about it, she agreed, just for peace and quiet. That night I could hardly sleep with excitement and at five the next morning Aggie came in, woke me up with a cup of tea and some toast and dressed me in a pair of shorts and tee-shirt. I kissed Mum and Dad goodbye and went out of the door holding Aggie's hand.

We seemed to walk for ages through dusty veldt, passing lots of thorn trees and mud huts with people sitting around their early morning fires, wrapped in blankets to ward off the dawn damp, which would later turn into a dry scorching heat. Now that I look back at this scene, I can imagine the sight that Aggie and I must have been to these observers; a little white girl holding a black woman's hand, walking through the bush at dawn. We got to her village, which in reality wasn't so far out of the main town, nor that far from our home, but to little legs it seemed in the middle of nowhere and a world away and far from anything I was used to.

On arrival at Aggie's collection of huts, where numerous family members lived, her children ran up to greet us with great excitement and took my hand and led me to their hut where they gave me water to drink in a tin mug. I was a great novelty to one and all. Aggie and the other adults started shouting amongst themselves and I realised they weren't quarrelling but just discussing the day's work ahead and that was just the way they talked. There were a few huts in a circle that belonged to various members of the family, but families in Africa were always growing and new huts were always needed and being built.

Everyone took off their shoes, me included, and we went into the hut that was being floored and knelt down on the rough floor that had been started some time ago. Aggie put down four or five big enamel floral basins with a browny reddish soft substance in all of them. She then showed me what I had to do: put my little hands into the goo, cup some out, put it onto the floor and then rub it into the surface in circular motions, so that the substance smoothed the rough texture of the ground beneath it. When all this was completed, the hut would be left open to the air and the floor would harden into a reddish, smooth even surface that would last for a lifetime, even with the daily sweeping with a hard reed broom, the scratching of the scrawny chickens looking for fleas, the continuous clawing of scavenging, mangy dogs and cats and innings and outings of many people over many years to come. I didn't know it then, but I do now, that things out there, were made with a purpose, made together for everyone, made to last and, more importantly, made with love. I can only guess and hope that, even now, that floor is still there.

What I didn't know at that time either, at least until the job was done, was that the substance we used on the floor was cow dung mixed with ox blood, bled from the animal's jugular vein when being slaughtered. I don't know whether knowing at the time that I was wallowing in the stuff would have changed my mind about helping Aggie or not. And when I say wallow, I really mean wallow, because by the time I was finished at the end of a very long day, I was covered with cow pooh and blood and I was as happy as I have ever been.

At midday Aggie washed me down and sat me under an old acacia tree with her brood of picaninnies and with the help of the older children, an old lady in a blanket and colourful *doek*, dished out tin plates of *mielie-pap* and a stringy meat stew to all of us workers. One of the old ladies told me that it was from an elephant that had been found dead after some ivory hunters had shot it for its tusks, leaving the body to rot. Fortunately, one of the men in the village had found it and the meat had been shared out. This old lady told me all this with a very straight face but I didn't know whether to believe her or not. But it was very tough and stringy meat, of a flavour I had never tasted before, so she may have been telling the truth. I ate it with gusto and couldn't wait to tell Mum and Dad that I had eaten elephant. I was told to roll little balls of *mielie-pap* in my hands and to dip them into the gravy and pop them into my mouth. I can remember being so hungry after all my hard work that no cat, dog, chicken nor fly got a crumb from my plate, much to the delight of all the African mamas sitting around that old tree.

After lunch, we sat around in the shade for a while, the adults talking or napping while we children played games, African games in the dust with stones and sticks, toys of the bush that gave pleasure and appreciation to the act and the word *play*. I felt like part of this family, part of their community. I felt love. These people had time for me, time to teach and show me things that I have never forgotten.

I can remember a few years later when I was playing with some white children in another part of the B.P., a little white girl asked the group of us playing together, "What do you want to be when you grow up?" One by one, they all answered that they wanted to be a nurse, a ballet dancer, a princess, the usual things little girls dream of being when they grow up. When she asked me I said, "I want to be black." Well, you can imagine what a stir that caused among those little friends of mine. "A black *what*?" they asked. "Just black," I said and I think that for me, it meant being something valid, belonging.

Anyway, after lunch under the acacia tree, we were told to go back into the hut to finish off the floor, which took most of the afternoon. At about five o'clock Aggie told everyone to finish off the job because she had to get me back home, otherwise the madam would be worried. She gave me a quick wash under the tap, saying that she would give me a good bath when we got home, but we had to hurry because the sky was getting very dark, as big purple clouds rolled overhead and the rumble of thunder could be heard in the not too far distance. On the way home the sky opened and we were under it. An African storm is spectacular; no storm anywhere in the world can compare to it. The rain came lashing down in heavy warm curtains of water, washing away all traces of dung and blood from my clothing, purifying me and cleansing me of the smell of death. When we got home, Aggie ran a hot bath for me and dropped my soggy clothes into the laundry basket, to be washed tomorrow, in the bath, bending over and scrubbing until all traces of dirt were gone, until her old back felt like breaking. She scrubbed me pink and rubbed me dry and glowing. When I was dressed in my pyjamas and slippers, sitting on the sofa telling Mum all about my day, Aggie made me a big mug of Ovaltine and hot buttered Bovril toast and I thought I had gone to heaven. The world had never, and has never, seemed so right.

*An Official Visit ~ and Me with Measles!*

The rain continued to fall the week after helping with Aggie's hut, washing all the dust away, exchanging it for mud. Everything smelt new and musty. The leaves on the trees turned from grey to various shades of green that had been hidden under drought's hues for far too long. This rain was another new adventure for me, never having seen Africa in the rain until now. The frogs sang and the birds were in a frenzy of delight, as all sorts of insects not seen before, came out of their hiding places and were washed up as gourmet delights, for beaks of different sizes to savour.

There was also another frenzy going on in our household because we were going to have an official visit from a bigwig from England, some government representative who I cannot recall anymore. Mum got some extra help in to get the house spotless and to relieve Aggie and Benson, who were put into the kitchen to help with the preparations for the official dinner. Mum and Dad had to entertain all sorts of people in their home as part of his job as District Commissioner.

In these far off stations, we were the only official representatives of the British government, so these visits were always a worry for Mum, who wanted it all to go off well. But it was never easy because there were no shops nearby and the entertainment allowance was pitiful, about twelve pounds a year Mum told me, so a lot of magic went into these do's and most of the allowance went on the booze.

The food was usually roast goat, the only animal that was plentiful in those parts, vegetables that came out of a tin and either a packet of chocolate angel whip, which we called *Kalahari Mud* or *364 Pudding*, which was fruit salad, so named because it was eaten three hundred and sixty four days of the year. This also came out of a tin, except in some places where we were stationed, where we had lovely fruit trees, but still it was eaten every day. Christmas day was the exception, when we ate Christmas pudding, sweating in the heat. Tradition was tradition and everyone got their Christmas pudding, either bringing it back with them while on overseas leave or on a trip to South Africa, where things were more civilised, especially the shopping. We got a big Christmas parcel from my grandmother in the Isle of Wight, containing presents for everyone, gentlemen's relish, stem ginger, special tins, chocolates and biscuits, crackers, stocking fillers, mince pies, a Giles cartoon book and the inevitable Christmas pud.

Anyway, back to the official visit, our first since arriving in Africa. Mum was to wear a suit she had bought from England with her, together with a pair of white gloves and a hat. All these outfits were stipulated on the list we were given before leaving the UK, together with regulation skirt lengths, rules and regulations on how to greet royalty, how to bow and curtsy and how to kiss a bishop's ring. Dad's outfit we called his 'ice-cream suit' because it was white from head to toe. His white trousers were topped by a white high-collared tunic-type jacket with gold buttons. His arms were restricted in movement because this whole ensemble was held in place by an overzealous Aggie, who starched this uniform until it stood up by itself and didn't need a coat hanger when Dad wasn't actually inside it. This outfit was completed by a white pair of shoes, whitewashed with much pride by Benson, and a pith helmet that covered Dad's eyes. I often wondered how on earth he could see where he was going. Then, to add a bit of colour to the finished outfit, there were his medals, earned for one thing or another, with their many coloured ribbons, attached to his chest.

The best bit of all was the sword worn by his side, with its shiny black scabbard and a huge gold tassel. When not on show for official colonial ceremonies, this sword was used on many less formal occasions to kill snakes – and did a very good job of decapitating them neatly and leaving the headless reptiles writhing around the yard, not knowing what had hit them. For every snake killed, a knot was tied in the tassled ribbon, keeping count. Looking at the beautiful, shiny sword on these very pompous occasions, one would never know what it had been used for behind the scenes. What I didn't know at that stage either, at the tender age of three, was that my father had the grand idea of using this very same sword for cutting my wedding cake one day.

The ice-cream suit was a source of great pride for Mum whom, I suspect, loved the snobbery of these occasions, but in truth this outfit did not suit Dad, simply because, although he was a good, highly respected and intelligent man, he was also very short. When I look back at the photos of him dressed up in his ice-cream suit, Mum very proud at his side, I have to smile.

Now came the question of what to do with me while this dignitary was on home turf. I was going to be allowed to watch the police- escorted cavalcade and then I had to be removed by Aggie to the back of the house, where I was going to be watched over by one of Aggie's family while she helped to serve at table, all bedecked in a new uniform, with Vaseline rubbed into her tribal marked cheeks to give her that extra sheen for this special visitor from overseas. I was not to be seen nor heard during the visit, because this was just for the grown-ups.

But fate had other ideas.

The day before the big occasion there was a frenzy of activity with colourful finery passing from white hands to black hands for laundering, altering, stitching, starching, polishing, airing and ironing. The delicious aromas coming from the huge cauldrons in the kitchen were mingling with the fragrances of cut flowers and the eternal smell of red floor polish and Benson's musty sweat, as he polished every inch of the floors until he could see his beaming face in the red-mirrored surfaces.

There were home-made soups, roast goat, several scrawny bush chickens on spits put up in the back yard, lots of colourful vegetables, some fresh, some tinned (frozen wasn't an option in those days in those places) freshly baked bread rolls, which were Aggie's speciality and, of course, 364 pudding and Kalahari Mud with evaporated tinned milk to pour over the whole lot.

There was as always, plenty of booze, which everyone appreciated more than the food and on these auspicious occasions everybody, regardless of rank, got as pissed as newts and what started out as a nervy occasion with everyone being very respectful and minding their p's and q's, usually ended up with everyone being everyone's buddy.

The next day there would be a lot of slagging everyone off and gossip amongst the neighbours who attended these do's and much hilarity in the kitchen, as the servants recounted what the big white bosses had got up to the night before, while they themselves had a whale of a time finishing off the rest of the food, the dregs in the glasses and a few bottles to boot.

On the big day I awoke with a terrible fever, a bright red rash all over my body and face and very red, sore eyes. Mum, being a nurse, recognised it straight away as measles but called the doctor over to look at me anyway and he confirmed her diagnosis. I was told to stay in bed, in a darkened room and to keep cool. I was considered a bloody nuisance, because everyone was too involved in the festivities to look after me. Mum would pop in every now and then to see me and Aggie would bring me freshly-squeezed lemon juice, but they would all just flit off again to attend to the business at hand and I felt very sorry for myself. Don't forget that we didn't have television, video or electronic games in those days. We didn't even have decent radio. There was an old box radio in the kitchen that gabbled on in Setswana, which Aggie and Benson listened to in the mornings.

So the short of it was, I was bored and lonely and didn't feel too well, but that wasn't the main problem for me.

I was going to miss all the fun.

It had been raining quite hard during the night, but the big day had arrived with beautiful blue skies, big white fluffy clouds tinged with purple, that could be an indication of further rain later on, to dampen the festivities and wash the spitted chickens of their crispy skins. I was hot and miserable in this dark prison of a room and I decided to go outside. Careful to avoid Aggie, Mum and anyone else likely to stop me, I climbed out of the window that led to the back garden, walked out of the back gate and into the bush behind our house. I knew where I was going to have some fun. There were a few enormous grey anthills behind our house, which were alive with huge red ants that stung like hell but when it had been raining, these ant heaps turned into a slippery slide. I climbed up one of them and slid down until I hit the ground with a bump. I slid down all of them and was enjoying myself until I heard a lot of noise, police sirens, hooting, a brass band and people cheering. I decided to investigate, being sure it was the cavalcade.

I was dressed in only a little pair of panties because that is what I had on while in bed, to keep me cool. Watching the official car in the distance escorted by policemen on motorbikes and followed by other cars carrying my father and other ice-cream suited gentlemen and their genteel, gaudily bedecked wives, waving white be-gloved hands at the natives, who in return waved little union jacks. Feeling the heat of the sun and the fever, burning me up and hardening the anthill clay all over my spots, I decided to take a dip in the huge puddle left by the night's storm that had filled a deep rut in the dirt road. At the bottom of the puddle I found an old condensed milk tin, so I filled it with muddy water and poured it over my head and the relief from the caked clay melting and the cool dirty water was delicious and what's more, I was having fun!

The crowd were watching me with amusement and laughing at my antics when suddenly the big black car stopped right in front of what I considered *my* puddle. The cavalcade could go no further, because I was in the way. A policeman asked me to get out of the road but I said no. The door of the official car opened slowly and this huge apparition stood over me. I blinked through the mud, as by this time, I was completely covered in a thick gooey mess and you could just see the whites of my eyes, although I should say the reds of my eyes, because they were so inflamed by the measles. What I was doing wasn't very good for me, to say the least.

The enormously fat man standing over me was encased in a dark navy uniform with gold buttons and array of ribbons and medals, rather like Dad's outfit but in navy blue and he seemed to be part of the suit, unlike Dad. The man's face was very red, due to the heat, being over dressed and probably gout, by the look of it, although I didn't know of such things at the time. On top of his silver head was a big navy blue hat with plumes on the top, very elegant and at the time, very frightening indeed.

"Well, well, well, what have we got here then?" he said in a booming voice, looking down at me with a twinkle in his very blue eyes.

By this time Dad had got out of the following car to see what the hold-up was and at the same time, Aggie had arrived on the scene, having been to my room and found me missing. Suddenly there was such a commotion, Aggie bowing to this gentleman and at the same time shouting at me and Dad telling me what a naughty little girl I was whilst trying to keep away from me splashing his nice, starched, white ice-cream suit.

I was whisked away by Aggie who had to change her uniform after handling her muddy charge and I was put into the bath and scrubbed, dowsed in calamine lotion and put to bed feeling sore, sick, sorry and elated at the same time. Nobody dared to smack me because I was sick, I am sure that had I been well, I would have had the biggest hiding of my life, the sort that parents aren't allowed to give their children today for fear of going to jail for it.

I was the subject of conversation at the dinner table and the guest of honour said that it was the best part of his official visit and that he had enjoyed it tremendously, as I had relieved the boredom that is so common at these functions. One by one, the guests came to my bedroom to see me and I suffered no side effects from my adventure. Aggie didn't want to talk to me the next day, she felt I had disgraced us in front of these important people, so I had to try and win her back, which took some time because she was a hard nut to crack, but I loved her.

Lobatsi wasn't the most exciting place to live and I was too young to remember much about it. After two years, we went on overseas leave to the UK, visiting grandparents, catching up on dentists and doctors check-ups and doing shopping for all the things we missed in Africa. We gave our cat to the doctor and Aggie promised to look after Jaggers for us, so we packed our goods and went on our way back home.

The boat trip was always a relief after the hot dusty villages we lived in, as the sea air was so fresh, clean and dust free. When we arrived in London, we usually stayed at the Overseas Visitors Club in Earls Court. This place was a haven for people from South Africa, New Zealand, Australia, Canada and elsewhere in the colonies. It was our stop over before continuing our trip to see the grannies.

The best part of the holidays, for me, was turning on the taps and having cool water splashing out of them or switching on the lights instead of having to light a paraffin lamp or candle. Such simple pleasures and yet such a novelty.

When our leave finished we were to go back to Africa, this time to a place called Kasane, by a big river.

However, before I take you to Kasane with me, I would like to share with you some descriptions of the features everyone who lives in Africa misses and never forgets.

## Descriptions of Nature

When I look at travel pamphlets, books, films, advertisements or any other medium that depicts Africa today, I feel a great nostalgic yearning but at the same time I recognise that it is not the same place I lived in. I was there before the tourists got wise to its beauty, when most people hadn't heard of a far-off place called Bechuanaland Protectorate. I consider myself very fortunate to have known a place unspoilt by so many of the damaging elements of the modern world.

My memories mix up my senses and the colours, sounds, sights and delights could be found in so many of the places I travelled through in those days. Before I take you onto our next village, I just want to share with you the delights of these senses which could be anywhere in Africa, but they were with me when I was a child, a little white picaninny and they are still with me now as a middle-aged woman living in Spain, so far away from the bush, and yet still so fresh in my mind.

## The Sky

There is no sky like an African sky. I have travelled all around the world and I have always looked up, comparing skies. Every sky is beautiful but the African sky is immense. When the sky is blue it is like looking up at a painting hanging upside down. When clouds start forming they roll in, white and fluffy, like huge cushions. There is nothing silent about the clouds over Africa, they seem to sing arias of great operas or talk as if they had something important to say. And they do, because the people are always waiting for much-needed rain, so they listen to what the clouds have to say. They listen to the music, just in case the tune changes. More times than not, these enormous, white, opera-singing clouds, just disintegrate and disappear, as if they had never existed in the first place. On those rare occasions that rain does actually manifest itself, those big white clouds turn mauve and purple, soon becoming navy then black and the rumbling begins, like the roar in a lion's throat. The animals get skittish and start darting in every direction and when the first drops of rain fall on the drought-stricken earth, there is no smell like it.

There was a village that hadn't had rain for twelve years, so some children had never seen rain their lives and didn't know what it was. They had only heard of it from the ancient ones tongues around the fires at night, together with all the other ancient tales passed down from generation to generation. One day the skies opened over this little dusty village and the surrounding areas and the rain fell, at first in big, soft, warm plops and then in sheets of water, white and cold, as never seen by the locals before. The old dried up riverbed filled and as the days went by and rain steadily came down without a break, the river broke its banks and flooded the village. The little mud huts were under water so that only their thatched roofs were to be seen from the overhead plane sent to survey the damage. Both people and animals tried to seek refuge by clambering on to these thatched peaks sticking out of the water. The crocodiles that had been hibernating under the old dried out riverbed now came alive, in one of Nature's miracles. These ancient creatures, driven by years of hunger, moved silently from rooftop to rooftop, picking off the stranded people and animals, helping themselves to the bounty that a very cruel Nature had provided.

Whenever you asked a native of a certain age from those areas when he was born, he wouldn't be able to tell you his date of birth, but he would be very proud to say, "I was born in the year of the great flood."

When the sun was high and hot, the sky lost its colour completely and became white and sizzled with a shimmering vibration that could be heard in the silence of midday in the bush. The sunrises and sunsets, either sitting on the banks of a river or in the middle of the Kalahari Desert, were always spectacular. The sounds of the animals stirring to look for food or a cool drink of water, the splash of the magnificent fish eagle as he hit the water and brought up a wriggling silver fish in his powerful talons, the different bird calls everywhere echoing on the breeze, the golden morning or evening glow on the backs of the shiny wet hippos as they wallowed.

The rainbows in an African sky are vivid, almost as if painted on a huge canvas. There are rainbows too on the spray of the Victoria Falls and in the spray made by the elephants as they have their evening bath.

The sky was always present in my mind as a child and seemed an important element. At night the same sky became another hive of activity. Night arrives suddenly and very quickly in Africa. There are the beautiful multi-coloured sunsets and then, wham, it's totally dark. The nights there are pitch-black. We used to sit in the garden after supper and look up at the night sky and it was beautiful because there were so many stars. The black sky above looked as though someone had scattered a million diamonds all over it and they had just clung there. Dad used to show me all the constellations and there were hundreds of shooting stars that we would wish on. There were also many UFO sightings, which doesn't surprise me at all, because the clarity of those unpolluted skies was beyond compare.

I used to love getting up early, at about five o'clock, before my parents awoke and slip out of the house and go to Aggie's hut, where she would brew me a tin mug of sweet tea, which I would sip around the early morning fire, shivering in the dewy air that would evaporate as soon as the sun came out and burnt everything in its wake. The steam from our mugs, the glow of the sun peeping over the thorn trees and the silence, broken only by bush noises, was, and still is, something I hold dear to me. We didn't need to talk at those times, we just were and that was enough.

## Water

There is never enough water in Africa, so it is worth more than gold. When something is scarce you notice it more, are more aware of it, although it wasn't as bad a situation as it is today. Our garden sprinklers always seemed to be on, giving us children great relief from the heat and endless hours of fun. We always had what we called a 'swimming pool' in our garden, which was usually a concrete square filled with green water which we shared with all sorts of animals. Some houses had what they called 'the reservoir', which was a huge round pool reinforced with corrugated tin and the water stored in these pools was used for the gardens, watered by the garden boy from a hose or a sprinkler.

We were lucky enough to live in two villages right on the river bank, which was wonderful because the river life was abundant and we never got tired of watching the very diverse and rich bird life, the aquatic animals like hippo and crocodiles, not to mention the antics of the little shiny brown bodies of the local kiddies, myself included, cavorting in the crystal-clear water. At sunset, when the whole bush turned crimson, the elephants would come down to the river to take a bath, while all the animals would line the banks, side by side, to slake their thirst, forgetting at that magical moment, that many of them were natural enemies.

My water memories are those of the rivers and the life surrounding them. The colours one would see as multi-coloured dragonflies and butterflies flitted past or in the wings of a scarlet-breasted shrike, or a bejewelled malachite kingfisher, or the iridescent flash of a starling as he swooped past. The brightly coloured frogs and insects, the colourful flora, the bobbing water-lilies, I could go on and on about the hues of the magical world of an African river bank. And all of these colours were magnified by the reflections of everything on the surface of the water, throwing it back at you, drawing you into what became a canvas of a real life painting.

Then, on top of this marvel of colour, you had the cacophony of sound. At rush hour on the banks of the river, there seemed to be every animal sound in the world, all the roaring, squeaking, squawking, scratching, honking and any sound ever made, you could find there. The hive of activity, of colour and sound was an entertainment that filled many an hour in my solitary childhood.

At times, usually during the hottest time of day, when animals slunk low, I would sneak out of my bedroom, unbeknown by Aggie and my mother, who thought I was having a rest as ordered. I would go down to the river, dressed only in a pair of panties and barefoot. Although I was dressed with Aggie's help in the morning, I would strip an hour or so later because I was a picaninny and didn't want clothes on at all. My feet were as hard as nails by now and nothing stood in my way, not the heat, nor fear of any beast at all. I would sit on the riverbank under a scorching sun and just contemplate all around me. I would be tempted to say that there was total silence and I suppose that compared to the rush hour of sunset there was, but within that hot white silence, there were always noises. There was clicking, gurgling, slurping and a thousand other noises that were going on all the time, made by the small creatures of the banks. They were lovely afternoons and far better than watching the telly.

The other water memories I have are of the mighty Victoria Falls in Rhodesia, as it was in those days. I remember the noise of all that mighty water, the permanent rainbow within its mists as the cascades fell in thundering crashes to the river below. We used to go to Rhodesia to do our monthly grocery shopping and we always stayed in a hotel close to the falls. I can remember sitting at the open air restaurant, under a canopy of huge trees, with an enormous oval platter in front of me, which was filled with a T-bone steak, sausages, chops, bacon, two fried eggs, fried bread, baked beans, grilled tomato and toast and to wash it down, a brown cow, which was a huge glass of coke with two balls of ice-cream thrown in. I can still feel the perfection of life as I sat in front of that plate of food, feeling the spray from the falls on my brown bare feet, while I shared my enormous meal with the monkeys that came down out of the trees from above, much to the annoyance of my parents, but I was in heaven.

The African storm is another element of water to be reckoned with. The sky in a storm is spectacular, the noise is incomparable, the thunder and lightning taking command of everything in its wake and after all the noise, it can sometimes frizzle out into nothing, leaving the bush a dust bowl, disappointing both beast and men. Or, it could culminate into a deluge, sheets of water coming down, painting over the dust to create new life. When the rain stops and the sun comes out, so do the animals, the insects and also the greenery and the beautiful array of multi-coloured flowers and all is well with the world again, abundance reigns and the smell of the bush after rain is magical, no perfume sweeter. After the rains, the bird song sounds clearer on the air and the cooing of the turtledoves mingle with the pecking of the woodpecker and the squawking of the vultures and the whole bush comes alive again with the cacophony of an African musical. Hail can sometimes come down in big balls of ice instead of the much-needed water and it is sad to see the thirsty animals licking these bits of ice, not understanding what they really are

Lightening is a real threat out there and I have lost two friends due to lightening. One of them was caught in a storm while out in the bush, so he sheltered under the only tree around which was a small thorn tree and as luck would have it, this tree was struck with him under it. The other man was sitting at a table in his hut having supper with his family, when lightning struck his hut just where he was sitting and it killed him out right. I am still very wary of lightening.

## Laughter

Africa has its unique sounds, from not only the voices, the chewing, snorting and munching of the diverse fauna of beasts and insects alike, of all sizes, but of the surroundings, whether it is by the river or in the middle of the Kalahari Desert. The breeze sings, the dust whispers, the trees rustle, seeds crack, sand shifts and the very heat sighs in anguish. All these noises are broken up by the often-heard death cries of a victim of nature, as another kill hits the ground running. The very silence of the bush crackles with an unheard buzz of activity. These noises one has to learn to listen to. I was lucky to have a Bushman gardener who taught me to listen to the silence and read its story on the wind.

African laughter is also a musical feast for the ears. Their laughter would rumble deep down in their stomachs and burst forth like a bubbling brook, full of joy and colour. The servants would stand at the bottom of their respective madams gardens and shout across the road to their friends working at other houses and their voices would carry all over the neighbourhood, floating on the still heat. Dad used to call it the bush telephone and it would annoy him on Sunday mornings when he wanted to have a lie-in and a conversation between maids would start up, making further sleep impossible.

## Smells

Africa smells different too. There is a musky smell on the air everywhere; it's a mixture of sweat, dust, exotic plants, hut-side fire smoke, cooking smells and animals. There was no pollution in those days so all that one smelt was natural aromas, belonging to the earth and to life. The river had a very distinct smell, a muddy, verdant, silty smell that clung to our hair after swimming in its waters, even after a shower. Aggie had a lovely smell to her. When I sat on her lap and she comforted me, I would put my head into her neck and breathe in deep. She smelt of cheap talcum powder, lifebuoy soap, starch and freshly baked bread, she also smelt of warmth and comfort, unlike Mum who always smelt of Lentheric Tweed and Lancôme. The smell of death also hovered everywhere, it was palpable. There was always an animal killing another animal, spilling and filling the air with blood and guts. The same went for man who had to hunt for food and often, just for fun, At least when it was an animal kill, there would be nothing left soon after the actual kill, because when the perpetrator had had his fill, the hyenas and other scavengers would do justice to the left overs, followed by the enormous vultures squawking and squabbling over the tit-bits. I used to love watching these huge birds at their meals and have always had a soft spot for them.

Man on the other hand, made his killing more obvious, more visual. When a beast had been shot, it was degutted, strung up, skinned, quartered and divided amongst many. There would be all these smells mingling with the perpetual dust, the blood and entrails, followed by the aroma of roasting meat on a spit. The skins would be salted and dried and that gave off a rank stink to it too, as did the biltong hung up to dry. Strips of meat would be salted, peppered, spiced and hung up to dry, giving off a whiff of its own, especially on a hot airless day.

The smell of fermenting marula fruit that lay rotting on the dry earth was almost like the smell of a rich brandied Christmas cake being baked in a hot oven. I loved marulas with their sweet juicy flesh that was slightly tart at the same time. I wasn't the only one who loved marulas. The baboons and elephants would feast on these fallen delights once they had fermented on the ground and they wouldn't stop at just a few, but would gorge themselves until they couldn't walk in a straight line, drunk as newts. It was very funny to see the apes falling out of trees because they couldn't hang on, having lost their grip. The elephants would stagger off into the undergrowth, bumbling blindly, not knowing where they were going, tripping over their flaccid trunks and crashing into trees as they went. The birds also behaved oddly after a meal of fermented fruit, trying to get off the ground with their wings flapping wildly, but nothing happening for them. I decided to try the bubbling fruit and although I preferred the fresh marulas, boy, did this stuff have a kick! It went straight to the head, powerful stuff for sure. Today, all over the world we can buy a marula cream liqueur but it's not half as nice as that hot bubbling stuff that lay in the dust for man and beast alike and free too.

*Tastes*

Food was hunted, fished, grown or came in a tin. We did most of our grocery shopping in Rhodesia once a month when we lived in Kasane. Whilst living in Lobatsi, Molepolole and Machaneng we made do with the little African stores and growing our own vegetables. We also got to know some of the wild vegetables that the Africans ate, like morogo, which is a wild leaf rather like spinach. Maun being a bigger village we had more shops, still little African or Indian stores, but more of them. The Maun of today has shopping malls, which is something I cannot even imagine. Anyone who hunted anything always shared their meat. There was an understanding that in these remote places everyone shared everything, it was a matter of survival. We always had scrawny looking chickens scratching around in the back yard. I had one called Susan and one day she disappeared, only to appear on my plate because Mum had had her slaughtered because we had no meat. It gave me great pleasure to note that she was as tough as old boots. We were lucky in Kasane because we had some good fish in the river and our garden had every fruit and vegetable imaginable. Aggie would get up early and pick big pink grapefruit for breakfast, squeeze fresh juice from our orange trees, make fresh bead rolls and collect fresh eggs from the hens, or buy fresh bream from a fisherman on the banks of the river. I can still taste those breakfasts that today we would call organic, but then, we called it survival. We also had strawberries, mangoes, pineapple, paw-paws, mandarins, loquats, bananas, peaches, plums, dates and every vegetable under the sun. The river was rich in nutrients and free of contamination, so everything that was planted grew in abundance. We didn't have fresh milk, cream or cheese, so we made do with tinned milk and packet whips. It was always a festive occasion when we went to Rhodesia for shopping because we would buy treats like chocolate, that although was all melty when we ate it, it made such a change from dusty, gritty lollipops.

I have eaten elephant, which I didn't know until afterwards when Aggie told me. When I ran crying to Mum to tell her she said it was my own fault for eating out the back with the Africans, instead of like a lady at the table. Although I was excited about eating elephant because it was something so magical eating one of those great beasts, I felt a deep-seated fear and a great sadness at the thought of what I had done. Today, I steer clear of meat. I can still remember the taste of mopane worms and flying ants and even crocodile and snake. But what I loved best was rolling little balls of mielie-pap in my hands and dipping it into a rich fatty sauce, just as the blacks did and I felt like one of them; food has never tasted so good.

## Colours

Some villages were pretty and some were desolate, but all were dusty and dry. After rain and the dust were laid to rest, everything would look prettier. The huts in most villages were built in a circle, with the chief's hut being bigger than the rest. There was always a fire outside the huts where all meals were cooked, tea was brewed and late into the black velvet nights, tales were told. If you took away the dust, you would see the colour of the beautiful plants, shrubs and trees. The colourful plumage and pelts of the animals, the coloured dresses of the women, the shiny nutty skins of the little picaninnies darting in and out of the water, all this comes to mind as I sit and reminisce. The African sky a continuously changing canvas, from white colourless heat, to violent reds, purples, oranges. The rivers, great, green and greasy, as Kipling described the

Limpopo, but sometimes, brown and moody, churned up by hidden beasts, or bruised and purple reflecting a brewing storm above. On days when the sky was picture- painted blue with a matching yellow sun, then the rivers resembled the sea with choppy little waves on the surface and reflecting all the jewelled colours of bird's feathers, overhanging trees, shimmering iridescent insects and life in all its glorious colour. On these clear diamond days, as I called them, the water was transparent and you could see all aquatic life below. The desert was a muted palette of pastel colours broken up here and there by patches of red earth. The plants were scrubby and low, with the occasional acacia thorn tree to break the skyline. The Kalahari was ugly and it was beautiful. It was noisy and it was silent, it was empty, it was seething. As the Bushman said, "you have to know how to listen and how to see."

# 4.  Kasane

Kasane is the meeting point of four countries, Botswana, Namibia, Zambia and Zimbabwe. In those days, it was in the middle of nowhere and that is where we were to live for the next two years. Mum was shocked once more because this place didn't even have one little store, nothing, zilch, just a house and a river. Next door was a dispensary for the basic health care of the natives.

Kasane was probably the best place we lived in, at least it was to me and it is the place that I have the most vivid memories of.

When we got to our new posting, Aggie was there to meet us and she had brought her older daughter Esther with her to help with the chores. Our house was the typical colonial abode that came with the job, an enmeshed veranda running around the house and front and back doors on spring hinges so that they couldn't be left open and let the snakes in, although they were always finding their way into the house despite the doors.

This house had a very big yard and at the bottom of the garden at the back, were the servants quarters, which were compiled of about four or five huts, much larger than we had in Lobatsi, which was nice for Aggie who, being far away from her village, would be bringing members of her family to stay for long periods and they would help around the house, becoming part of our family.

The garden was a real Garden of Eden, with every fruit and vegetable under the sun and as I mentioned in the previous chapter, everything grew well. We had a small rusty wire fence around the property, which was useless at keeping anything out at all. From our stoep we could see the river, which was about two minutes', walk away from the house and it was a lovely lookout spot. Next door to the right of our house, another similar house was allocated to the local policeman. To our left was the local dispensary that I mentioned before and that would save Mum from dying from boredom. The man who ran this place was a lovely black man called Duncan and he welcomed Mum with open arms when he heard that she was a nurse. She never was paid for helping out in the clinic, but she enjoyed it tremendously. I will go into more detail later on about the dispensary.

Aggie and Esther managed the house well between them and we didn't have a man around the place as we did in Lobatsi, that is, until Txao came into our lives.


## Txao

One day when we went into the garden after breakfast, we saw a man sitting at the bottom of the garden whittling a piece of stick. He had an old felt hat with holes in on his head and very ragged clothes. His face was as wrinkled and dry as the drought stricken earth of the Kalahari and he only had a few brown teeth left in his head, but it was his eyes that were the lights in his face. When he looked at you, it was as though he knew everything and had been around since the earth came into being. When he smiled the lines on his face shifted like the desert sands and his eyes disappeared altogether, it was the smile of the sun. Through Aggie, we asked him what he wanted and he said that his name was Txao and he wanted a job as gardener. When he spoke, it was in the clicks of the Bushman, which Aggie understood. His words floated on the breeze like an ancient musical instrument. As the garden was so big and we needed to grow most of our food, Mum employed Txao and he was given one of the huts in the yard. Although he accepted the hut, he would disappear into nowhere for long periods at a time and nobody knew where he got to. Although he did his disappearing acts sometimes, Mum couldn't fault him on his job because the garden blossomed and bloomed continuously, without ever stopping. This man had magic fingers. I was fascinated by Txao and would follow him around all day. He would talk to me in his click language all the time and tell me stories in his tongue that I couldn't understand, but loved listening to for the musical clicks. He would gesticulate with his slim wizened fingers, trying to make me understand the stories of his world, which judging by his wild gestures, were all about animals. I could now speak a fair amount of Setswana, especially the swear words, but I could never master the clicks. Txao also made me little wood carvings of wild animals, which he would incorporate into these epic stories that I loved listening to. When we left Kasane two years later, he gave me a Bushman bow and quiver full of poisoned arrows, which I still have at home today, over fifty years later.

## Esther and My First School

Esther was a lovely, polite and bright girl, or so I heard Mum say more than once. I loved her like an older sister and she looked after me as though I belonged to her alone. Not far from our house, an enterprising young man had started a school for the little picaninnies, to teach them the basics of counting, reading and writing. Ester helped the teacher with the little ones while he concentrated on the older ones. She asked Mum if she could take me with her and Mum delighted to get rid of me for a bit of peace and quiet, agreed. I was so, so excited about the fact that I was going to go to school for the first time in my life, at the ripe old age of nearly four. On my first morning, Aggie dressed me in a little pink dress and flip-flops and after breakfast Ester came into the house to collect me. I can still remember walking down that dust rutted path amongst the thorn trees, holding Esther's hand, my little pudgy, sweaty, pink hand in Esther's cool, slim, brown one. After walking a bit we came to a clearing that was surrounded by grass huts. In the middle of the clearing was an enormous baobab tree that went up into the sky, at least to a tiny tot, it seemed that way. The trunk of the tree was completely hollow, with a doorway into it. The baobab formed a lovely leafy roof over the clearing and this was the place that the elders of the village held their kgotlas, or meetings, to discuss village business. It was the place where the mamas would sit in the heat of the afternoon, when their chores were finished and gossiped. It was also our school. Inside the trunk all the teacher's equipment was kept. That equipment consisted of an old blackboard on an easel, several little slates and pieces of white chalk and an old abacus with very worn coloured beads. The little picaninnies got very excited when they saw me coming to their school and Esther had to tell them to behave themselves, but all through that first day the giggles were the highlight of the event and are still with me to this day. I didn't have the feeling of being ridiculed, as I did later on in the schools I went to. The giggles of my little brown friends were giggles of friendship, shyness and novelty. I was given a slate and a piece of thin chalk and we were away, on the path to greater things, I was at last at school, even though it was in a baobab tree, the best school I have ever been to. At break we had to stand in line while Esther washed our hands with water from a gourd and then we were all given a large seed pod from the baobab tree and inside were white woolly seeds that we sucked and they tasted of lemon drops. After playing and running around in the dust for a while, we went back to class until midday. At lunchtime Esther and I walked home hand in hand, under the searing heat. I was anxious to tell Mum and Dad all about my first day and also to take off my itchy dress and run around under the sprinkler, rejoicing in the simple joy of living.

## The Jail

One of Dad's functions in his job was to try criminals. In Kasane we had a jail and it was always full. Crimes consisted of stealing livestock, wives and children, usually for witchcraft which was rife and murder. The prisoners were let out during the day to clean the dusty rutted roads and pathways and the river bank and other jobs like cutting trees, cleaning up the district commissioner's garden, the odd paint job and whatever else that needed doing around the village. These men were guarded by a couple of policemen all the time, rather like the chain gang in America. They sang while they worked and were always laughing. Unlike the American version that one sees in the movies, these men had no intention of escaping and were not chained, in fact quite the opposite situation was the problem. When these men finished their days work they were escorted back to their jail for the night. The jail doors, although locked, really didn't have to be, because the prisoners loved being in jail and often the policemen would leave the doors open and wander off somewhere and on returning would find all men still there. In many cases, when a prisoner had served his time and was released, he would be back a couple of weeks later, having committed another crime. Dad was perplexed about this and decided to investigate. What it boiled down to, was that the men were so happy and contented with life in jail that they didn't want to be on the outside. They got three good meals a day, a clean uniform, free cigarettes, a present at Christmas, work outside in the fresh air every day, where they could chat to passers-by and their families could visit them too. Most of them had a far better life inside than out.

### The Dispensary

Duncan ran this little clinic by himself, at least until Mum came along and gave him a hand. It consisted of two rooms in a mud building with a tin roof and then there was a couple of round, thatched, mud rondavels, with a couple of beds in them for the bad cases. There were the basic mutis or medicines and Duncan did what he could with very little. There was always a trickle of people coming to the clinic with ailments and some would walk great distances to get there. I remember a few cases that stood out among the rest.

A pregnant woman walked, almost staggering into the dispensary grounds one day, obviously exhausted. There were quite a few people sitting outside in the grounds under the shade of the trees, while the scrawny chickens scratched in the dust around them. Everyone sitting outside was waiting to see Duncan and Mum with their ailments. They were drowsy with the heat and the boredom of waiting, when this heavily pregnant woman staggered into the yard and collapsed. Everyone went to her aid and called Duncan who came out with Mum to see what all the fuss was about. Between a couple of men they managed to get her inside and on to the examining table. They revived her and gave her a cup of water because she was obviously extremely thirsty. She told Duncan that she had walked for eighty miles and that she was very tired. When she had started labour pains, she decided to leave her village and walk to the dispensary. She had walked the whole eighty miles in labour and was fully dilated when she arrived. Duncan tried to get her to push to expel the baby, but the woman had gone into a deep sleep and she slept through the whole birth process, only awakening when it was all over, to be told that she had a healthy baby boy. Mum tried to get the woman to have a meal and recover before returning to her village, but the woman was adamant that she had to get back as soon as possible, so she put her new born on her back, tied with a blanket and started on her eighty mile trek back home.

There was another birth that caused a stir for Mum. Duncan wasn't there that day as he had to go out to a remote village to see a sick old man and Mum stayed at the clinic doing what she could with Aggie as interpreter. A woman came in with a lot of family members and she was obviously in labour, so Mum and Aggie went about delivering the baby who arrived shortly afterwards. When the afterbirth was expelled, Mum took it and was about to dispose of it in the boiler when the paternal grandmother started shouting and threatening Mum and all the other family members started joining in and they got quite violent. Aggie had taken the baby out of the room to wash it, so Mum was alone with this ugly scene and not understanding what they were shouting at her she was really afraid that they might hurt her. Luckily Aggie came in before Mum got rid of the afterbirth and she explained that the family wanted it to take home with them because they were going to eat it. Mum said they couldn't do that, it wasn't right. Aggie explained that it was a tradition and had magical properties. So the afterbirth was wrapped up in an old newspaper and handed over to the agitated old woman and everyone was happy, everyone except Mum that is and she didn't want any lunch that day, but she was learning. In that part of the world there are a lot of women walking around that area called either Susan after me, or Evelyn after my mother, after being helped in labour by Mum.

One day a very thin young man came to the dispensary and said he was going to die on the first of April, a week away. Duncan examined him with Mum and they couldn't find anything wrong with the man, except that he was very dehydrated and emaciated. They put him to bed in one of the huts to keep him under observation. Aggie would take plates of food over to him from our house, but on returning an hour later found the food untouched and this went on for a couple of days. He would never say why he wouldn't eat. The biggest problem of all was that he wouldn't drink either and he was getting weaker by the day. The first of April was looming and the man was dying and Mum was desperate. She got Aggie to pick some oranges off our tree and squeeze a jug of juice, added some sugar and lots of ice and she took a tray with a tall glass and the jug of juice over to her patient. When he refused to drink, she told him that the great white queen from across the water drank this miraculous drink and it gave her great power. At this news the man blinked and he struggled to sit up, so Mum helped prop him up on the pillows. He asked her if what she had said was true and Mum assured him that it was gospel truth. The man took a sip and then glass after glass was drunk until the jug was empty. Mum had broken the spell. Apparently, this young man had gone to a witch-doctor for some treatment for a minor ailment and he couldn't afford to pay the witch-doctor who had given him a deadline for payment. When the deadline arrived and payment was not met, the witch-doctor told the young man that he would die on the first of April and so the man was convinced that he was going to die and he would have too, if he had continued not eating and drinking. The fact that the powerful white queen over the water took this drink, made him think that if it did her good, it must be pretty powerful stuff. Witchcraft in Bechuanaland was rife in those days.

Duncan and Mum also looked after a leper colony not far out of the village and I used to go along with them in the truck when they did their weekly check-ups there. I would play with the leper children and it fascinated me to see their mutilated little bodies, but it did nothing to stop us playing together, the simple, dusty games of innocent children who accepted each other just the way we were.

## Trips

Dad would often have to go into the bush with a policeman to outposts to sort out local problems. There were some times that Mum and I went with him which was fun because we would see lots of wild animals and new faces. Although we saw a lot of wild animals just sitting at home and the faces we saw on our trips were similar to the faces we saw at home too, but it was fun. For these trips we would stock up the scoff- box, which was a huge big green metal trunk, which we would fill with the basics like tea, coffee, sugar, salt, dried milk and lots of tins that would make a bush stew with added potatoes and onions at the drop of a hat, as soon as we stopped to make a camp before the sun set at the end of each day. We had a driver called Jack who did all the official driving for the Government and he drove a caboose. This huge vehicle was like an old fashioned pop band's motor-home. It was very big, very grey and very metallic and military looking, with enormous wheels. Inside were beds and a table and lots of cupboard space. This thing could go everywhere and drive over anything, nothing would ever get in its way and it never got stuck in the sand which was always a problem for lesser vehicles. We had a variety of cars and trucks while we lived in Africa, but the best was the caboose, which although wasn't really ours, we used it a lot, with Jack at the wheel and an old grey Land Rover which, although very uncomfortable, was extremely reliable. Jack was a coloured man, not black, not white, but a lovely golden colour, with a little moustache. He originally came from the Cape and he was well known throughout the country, not only for his bush skills, but for his lovely humour and friendliness.

I can remember on one of these trips, something happened that made Dad a God in the eyes of the locals. We got to this small village with the circle of little thatched huts and the clearing with a big tree in the middle, which as usual, is the village city hall where all social and political events take place. Jack parked the caboose under some shady trees and put the kettle on to brew some tea for us all, while Dad went in search of the chief. As there was a serious drought in the country that was affecting everyone badly, amongst other lesser problems, the main agenda for the kgotla that day, was seeking solutions to the problems the drought brought with it. Some children in the village had never seen the rain. After tea, Dad went off to join the chief and all the village elders. All the men sat in a circle facing Dad and the chief. Mum and I watched the proceedings from the caboose while Jack had a nap under a thorn tree, with his hat over his face. The day was very hot with a searing white sky above and not a cloud in sight. In the midday heat the stick-thin dogs lay in whatever shade they could find, under swarms of drowsy bluebottle flies. These flies were everywhere in thick clouds, which neither man, woman, child, nor dog, had the energy to shoo away from eyes and mouths. The dust laced heat made it all too much of an effort. The afternoon was drowsy and silent, apart from the droning voices from the kgotla drifting across the clearing, with the heat carrying the murmurings out into the surrounding scrubby grey bush. Mum and I soon got sleepy with heat and boredom and dropped off too, waiting for Dad to finish his meeting. It was a custom in these parts of the

BP, that when a kgotla ended, all the men stood up and in unison shouted "PULA!" which means rain, because rain is such an important element there. Mum and I had woken up when we heard all the old men shuffling to their feet, indicating that the meeting was coming to an end. They all put their arms in the air, reaching for the sky and Dad shouted at the top of his voice, "PULA!" and suddenly, out of nowhere, the heavens opened and down came the rain, the first for many years and oh boy, it poured down. Everyone in the village started shouting that Dad was a god and that this was a true miracle. Dad had to hotfoot it to the caboose as quickly as possible, shouting at Jack to get the hell out of there *tout suite* before the villagers made him the new chief and dressed him in animal skins with a bone put through his nose. Whenever he went back to that village, he received the best welcome any white man ever had anywhere in Africa.

### Crocodile Wilmot

On one of our trips to Rhodesia to get our monthly groceries, we took Aggie and her newest baby boy of two, Pilwently. Although Aggie looked as old as the hills and didn't know her age, she was obviously still willing and able to give babies and all with different men, none of whom we met while we were living in the B.P. And as the staunch Roman Catholic she professed to be, she didn't use any contraceptives and all babies were welcome. We had had a lovely shopping trip and had stayed at the Victoria Falls hotel, so we were feeling very jolly. We had taken the caboose with Jack as driver this time. Usually we went in a Chevy truck, but because Aggie wanted to come with her baby too, we thought that the caboose would be more spacious.

On our way back home to Kasane, about four hours out of Rhodesia, there was a horrible noise in the caboose and then it stopped dead. Dad and Jack got out to investigate and found that the fan-belt had broken. There was very little traffic on those dusty bush roads in those days, so the only thing for it was for Dad and Jack to walk back to Rhodesia. They decided to go together for safety, leaving Mum, Aggie, Pilwently and me with the caboose.

We made tea, ate a lot of the goodies we had bought in Rhodesia, melted chocolate and bright green jelly crystals straight from the packet. We played 'I Spy' and other guessing games until we were fractious and boredom set in. The heat was unbearable, the air didn't move, the sun was high in the sky, the hours ticked by slowly, Pilwently screamed, I whined, Aggie threatened and Mum was desperate. We were a sorry-looking little group in the middle of the bush. In desperation, Mum made us a fizzy drink with tepid water from the canvas water bag hanging off the side mirror of the caboose and Alka Seltzer; not the best tasting drink in the world but it was a novelty and tickled our noses. It was all we had at hand, because all the pop and juice was right at the bottom of all the groceries with other things on top and it was all packed in such a way that to go searching for it would take ages and to pack it all away again would take even longer.

Then Mum had another brilliant idea, at least she thought it was a good idea, to amuse us kids. She had always been a natural blonde but had wanted a change, so while in Rhodesia she had bought red hair dye to use at home. She got out the box of dye and started mixing it with more of the tepid water and when she was sure it was the right consistency, she started painting this virulent scarlet all over her hair with the little brush that came with the dye.

Aggie clicked her tongue and muttered obscenities under her breath that Mum didn't understand but which I did. All the while Mum was applying the dye, she was clowning around pulling funny faces and singing. Her idea was to stop Pilwently screaming and me whining and we did, both of us stopped dead in our tracks, gawping at Mum as though she was stark raving mad, which is what Aggie thought.

I wasn't sure whether it was my mother acting crazy or the fascination of this bright red goo on her head that took my mind off our predicament and I wasn't sure either what little Pilwently thought, because he just stared wide eyed at Mum, then looked at me and back at Mum again, as though trying to figure out what on earth had changed. At least silence reigned, for about ten minutes, that is. Mum said she had to wait for half an hour and then she would rinse the colour off under the tap at the side of the caboose, "and when daddy comes back he will find a beautiful new mummy". But as I said, ten minutes into the completion of applying the dye we heard the familiar trumpeting of elephants in distress. Looking around the caboose we saw a big herd of these magnificent beasts just standing in front of our vehicle and it was obvious that we were in their way. There were several enormous adults, all flapping their ears, swinging their trunks and pawing the ground, raising huge clouds of dust and with them were a couple of babies that were being surrounded now by the protective family in the face of danger.

Now, I have never worked it out whether the danger to those beasts was the big grey caboose that looked like another elephant or the raving mad Englishwoman with a dripping scarlet head. Aggie went into the caboose and came out with the new tin saucepans and lids that she had bought in Rhodesia and started banging them together creating a hell of a noise. The elephants started trumpeting even louder and then there was the sounds of gunshots above the animal noise and all chaos broke loose.

We didn't know where the shots came from and we couldn't see very much with the swirling dust the elephants were kicking up. They were turning around in a circle and started moving off into the bush, leaving us in peace, still with our stomachs in knots, dust in our eyes and stuck on the lollipops that Pilwently and I were sucking at the time of the skirmish. Another of many dusty lollipops. Mum's red dye was covered in dust and dripping down her face in rivulets, looking like she was a victim of a horrible bloody crime.

Through the dust we saw a couple of men walking towards us dressed in khaki safari suits and felt hats on their heads, both carrying big hunting guns. When they saw Mum they stopped in their tracks and just stared and then they burst out laughing at this mad sight. The older man introduced himself as Wilmot. He was leather skinned, blue eyed and grizzled by life in the bush, a professional hunter. The other man was his assistant. They had been coming back from Rhodesia when they came upon the herd of elephants up ahead of them and as they couldn't move, they got out and found the herd was stopped by us, so all in all, we were the problem for man and beast. They fired into the air to frighten the elephants off.

Introductions were made and Mum explained what had happened to us and did her best to explain why she looked the way she did. Wilmot then went back to look for Dad and Jack. He found them, took them into Rhodesia to buy a new fan-belt, then brought them back to the caboose where the vehicle was fixed and we could get on our way back home. While these two men had gone in search for Dad, Mum did her best to rinse the dye out of her hair, but due to all the fuss, the dye had stayed on far too long and the water in the caboose tank was scarce. By the time Dad came back, Mum looked like a frightened carrot with matching drips down her face. Dad said she looked beautiful but I don't know whether it was because he was the eternal English gentleman, too afraid to say anything that may whip up her Welsh temper, or simply that he didn't even notice the change, because Dad was like that. From that day, Wilmot became a good friend and many years later, when writing his memoirs, he wrote that of all his bizarre experiences in the bush, coming upon a strange English lady dripping red hair dye, surrounded by herd of angry elephants, with two kiddies, one black, one white, sitting on the bonnet of a caboose sucking big multi-coloured gobstoppers while a crazed African woman banged pots and pans together, had to beat them all!

The banging of pots, pans and tins was a sure way to get the great beasts to move off without hurting them and we used this method often whenever we were confronted with elephants. The trouble came when you didn't have a saucepan with you. Not many folk walked through the bush with their kitchenware, but we did, just in case.

## Elephants, Hippos and other Dinner Guests

Elephants were plentiful in those days and we would see them often. I remember one morning when Dad tried to open the front door to go to work couldn't budge it because there was an elephant sitting on the doorstep. Our garden was an Eden for animals because they loved the fruit trees and vegetable garden. Many a time you would lie in bed and hear munching and when you went to investigate, would find a couple of hippos going down the rows of veggies, eating everything in sight.

## Charged by a Bull Elephant

One day we went to visit a Greek friend of Mum and Dad's who lived a few hours away from where we lived. This man was a dentist in Rhodesia but lived in the bush with his wife and son, who was a couple of years older than me. Whenever we needed a dentist we went to him in Rhodesia but this time it was just a social visit; we were going to stay for lunch and come back in the evening. Although Dad sometimes had no choice about driving when it was dark, he preferred not to, so we always tried to get back before nightfall, unless we were asked to stay overnight, which, work permitting, we sometimes did. Driving at night was scary because African nights are pitch-black and there are no streetlights. There were no proper roads to talk of and the bush all looks the same, unless you are a Bushman and know how to read it. As you travel over bumps, you never know if you've ridden over an animal or just a rut in the road. The bush is full of glowing lights, which are really the eyes of all the animals out on the hunt. Some glow green, others gold or even red, like sparkling jewels flashing past the truck. The best time to travel at night is under a full moon because that lights up the whole bush, giving off a glow that lights your way, showing you the purple shadows of the animals stalking their prey under the navy blue acacias; it's magical. But on a moonless night, you can see nothing at all; you can only hear the night.

After we had had a specially prepared Greek lunch, the adults sat around and continued drinking and chatting, while George and I went out to play. We were warned not to go too far because there was a storm brewing and the sky was rumbling, with flashes of lightning tearing at the deep purple clouds above.

Our friend's house was in a very isolated place and although their fenced property was surrounded by cultivated vegetation, once you went out of their yard you could see for miles around, right up to the distant horizon. The view was just scrubby plains broken up here and there by acacia trees and the occasional baobab and sky looked immense above this barren panorama.

George and I went out of the yard, as he wanted to show me the wreck of an old plane that had crashed in that area a couple of years previously. We walked for what seemed ages and, as we walked, the house got further away; by the time we got to the plane, all we could see was a speck in the distance like a little doll's house.

We got into the wrecked plane and played that we were flying high above and going to all sorts of exotic places. The wind started howling around us, the sky became darker, the thunder got closer and we could see jagged flashes of forked lightening in the distance, but we didn't care about the storm, nor our parents' warnings, we were having a whale of a time! But then we heard it, that unmistakable sound that echoes throughout Africa, the trumpeting of a furious elephant. We stopped making engine noises with our lips and sat in silence, looking at each other, not daring to move. From where we sat we couldn't see anything, so we squeezed ourselves out of the rusty cockpit and jumped down out of the plane. Then we saw him – and what's worse, he saw us. This beast must have smelt us before seeing us and when he did spy us hiding behind the old wreck, all hell broke loose.

This was the biggest bull elephant I had ever seen or have ever seen to this day. He had enormous tusks, which he was lancing upwards towards the black sky as he bellowed and trumpeted. He pawed at the swirling dust, which rose up in clouds around him. His huge battle-torn ears flapped, not only from the howling wind, but from an anger deep inside him. This elephant was magnificent but also very, very mean and so very angry at the brewing storm. He wanted to take it out on something or someone and that someone was us; two little innocent kiddies, far from home.

George and I took one look at each other, one look towards the house in the distance and started running for our lives. When the elephant saw us running, he put his ears back and charged after us. As he gained on us, we could hear the earth tremble with each of his steps. There was rumbling from the thunder above and rumble from the ground below and we were in the middle. I have never felt so much panic in my life.

The house didn't seem to get nearer, but the elephant did, from behind. I could feel a deep searing pain in my chest as I ran and a stitch in my side from sheer exertion. I didn't cry but my eyes were streaming from the wind and the dust as we sped across those plains trying to get to safety, before the elephant got us.

Just before we reached the house, the skies opened, the rain poured down and there was silence, only the sound of the water hitting the parched earth, no wind howling, no thunder rumbling and no elephant trumpeting or stomping. We stopped to look back and saw that the elephant had stopped too. The rain had done something to calm him. He stood there, in front of an old acacia tree, a silhouette against the evening sky, black and gleaming under the rain, washed free of the grey dust. He shook his enormous noble head and looked up at the sky, almost like praying, thanking his primitive Gods for the relief of rain.

George and I ran inside the yard and shut the gate, collapsing on the step, unable to breathe. When we got our breath back, we started laughing like hyenas and promised never to tell the parents. It was to be our secret, just as so many of the things I did in the bush were secrets.

## Bushman Drums

The sights, smells and sounds were different in Kasane from what they were in Lobatsi because Kasane was more isolated, more in the bush. In Lobatsi the population was bigger and there were more cars and shops. When we first got to Kasane we noticed the sounds of silence, broken only by nature's interference. As a child of four, something bothered me terribly; in fact, it scared me quite considerably. I would lie in my bed at night clenching my fists and lying as stiff as a board, trying not to breathe too loud, or to move, just in case I missed the sound, because I felt that if it stopped, then 'they' were on their way to get me. What frightened me to death between those sweat-soaked sheets – pulled right over my head, no matter what the temperature – was the drumming. Every night the drums would start and as the night wore on it would get louder. I even imagined that they were right under my window.

I had never been a scaredy-cat and during the day I wandered all over the bush by myself, dressed only in a little pair of panties and no shoes. I picked up every animal, insect and snake that crossed my path and prodded every mushroom and plant I came across, without thinking about the dangers lurking in every corner of the bush. I really think that I had a guardian angel watching over me, or maybe it was an African sprite. I was a real little tomboy and as tough as they came, but the drumming worried me. I called Mum into my room umpteen times every night and although she heard them too she didn't seem too worried about them, saying, "don't worry about them love, they are across the river and they won't hurt you". But that explanation didn't help ease my mind in the least, so I thought that the only thing to do about it was to investigate.

So one very hot day, after breakfast, I wandered down to the riverbank and, as luck would have it, there were a couple of mokoros at the water's edge. A *mokoro* is a long canoe-type boat dug out of a tree trunk and it is used by the natives for moving around the rivers and for fishing. A long pole is used to push the boat along by putting the pole into the water until it hits the bed of the river and then when pushed, it propels the boat forward, rather like a punt or a gondola.

The river was wide and teeming with crocodiles, hippos and a lot of other wildlife but that didn't worry me. I could see the other side of the river and also knew how to swim, so with all the cocky confidence in the world, I got into the mokoro, pushed away from the bank with the pole and away I went on my adventure, to find the drums. I had lain awake the night before, planning what I would do if I found the drummers. I didn't think they would eat me because Aggie had told me that white people don't taste very nice. I'm not sure how she knew but some questions were better not asked. I would tell them very nicely that their drumming was keeping me awake and would they be so kind as to not bang so loud. If they got nasty, I would resort to nasty tactics myself and tell them that Dad would put them in jail. I had it all sorted in my mind and was convinced that I couldn't fail in my mission.

Oh, the innocence of children!

The crossing was hard going for a little girl and I was lucky that we hadn't had any rains recently to swell the river to depths that would have made my crossing impossible. My mokoro zigzagged across the water in a very helter-skelter manner due to my size and inexperience. I had seen little boys not much older than me manoeuvre these vessels all by themselves, but they had been born to it.

There wasn't anyone else on the river that day and I was sweating with the effort of getting the mokoro to the other side.

There were a few crocs floating just below the surface of the water and quite a few lying around on the sandy banks sunning themselves and there were also occasional little ears of submerged hippos breaking the surface every now and then, but they didn't seem very bothered by my intrusion into their world. The best thing about being on the river was watching the birds dipping into the water. The majestic fish eagle swooping down for a catch, the kingfishers and shrikes, among many others in gaudy feathers, flitting past and all calling out in their different voices. All of nature's activity made me feel that I was among friends and not at all alone in the middle of a river.

Eventually I got to the other side of the river. I cannot remember how long it took me, but I had made it. I jumped out, pulled and pushed the mokoro onto the sand and went in search of the drums. The bush was very dense here and there were no houses at all. I waded through the vegetation, brushing branches out of the way so that I could get through. All around me was closed in by foliage and the only opening was the blue sky above if I looked up. Eventually I heard voices, so I followed the direction they came from and suddenly, there before my eyes, were a group of little naked golden people. I say 'golden' because they were not black like Aggie or the other Africans we had come across, except for Txao.

There was a silence when the group saw me and they looked at each other and then at me, covering their mouths with their knarled claw-like little hands, ancient hands. Then they all started chattering at once, not Aggie's language, but Txao's – Bushman. There were a lot of shrieks and whoops, giggling and clicking; I had obviously caused quite a stir. They inched closer to me, bit by bit, and one by one they touched me and jumped back as though I would bite or sting them. They were afraid of me. I wasn't afraid, I was just bemused, to say the least. They pulled my hair, trying to feel it; they prodded my belly and smacked my bum playfully, having such fun at my expense. I tried to talk to them in Setswana, telling them about the noise their drums were making at night, but I could have been talking to a stone, they didn't understand me at all.

One of the women brought me a gourd filled with wild honey and indicated to me to drink it. I sat on a rock and started to drink the honey under the watchful eye of the whole Bushman tribe, men, women and children. The honey was very sweet and full of locusts, flies and other dead insects that were considered a good nutritional source by these people. I can still remember the honey running down my chin and onto my fat, round, suntanned little tummy. I had honey everywhere, even in my hair, much to the delight of my new friends.

As I was finishing off my treat, Aggie burst through the undergrowth, swearing and shouting and threatening me with the beating of my life. She pulled me off the stone and started smacking me on the backside. At that moment, all the Bushmen moved in between her and me and tore her off a strip. Bushmen don't ever hit their children and they weren't going to let Aggie hit me. When Aggie calmed down, I told her why I had come and about the drums frightening me at night. She translated this to the Bushmen and they started laughing and told me not to be afraid and that they were my friends and they would bring me gifts to show me that they were my friends. They told Aggie that although they knew that white people were around, they had never seen a white person before; I had been the first one. Aggie muttered under her breath, in English, that these people were savages. I said goodbye to my new friends and Aggie yanked my sticky little hand in hers and took me back to where the mokoros were on the riverbank.

When Mum and Aggie had noticed me missing, Aggie had gone down to the river because a passer-by had told her that he had seen me heading that way. Aggie, having sixth sense, guessed where I had gone and decided to investigate herself, taking the other mokoro and crossing the river. At first she thought that I may just have gone a little way up our side of the river, but on not finding me, she went across and tracked me down. She didn't stop shouting at me all the way home, her voice echoing all the way up the river, frightening all wildlife in our path. When we got home, Dad was waiting for me because Mum had called, him saying that I was missing. I got a hiding that day and was locked in my room without any supper. I don't know why they were so worried that time. I had gone to a lot of far-flung places in the bush before, without them worrying, but I guess Aggie had a lot to do with it and I hated her for it too. That night I lay in my bed and listened out for the drums and sure enough, they started up and got louder as the night wore on, but I wasn't afraid anymore, they were my friends and the sound was comforting. Maybe that hiding was worth all the trouble I had gone to feel safe and unafraid.

The next morning when I went outside, on the door-step was an ostrich egg, a gift from my Bushman friends, just as they had promised. And every morning there was a gift for me. They left a beautiful little miniature courting bow, with a quiver of tiny arrows. These are used when a young man wants to wed a young girl, he shoots the tiny arrows into the front of her hut and if she collects them it means he has been accepted, but if she leaves them, then he knows he has to look elsewhere. They also left freshly hunted meat, freshly caught fish, animal skins, musical instruments, nuts and berries, jewellery made by themselves out of all sorts of seeds, shells and plants, feathers and so many of their treasures. I was truly blessed by these beautiful people and have carried them in my heart since then.

The Bushmen listen out for the rain bird because this bird has a call that sounds like water running over stones and when this bird calls, the Bushmen follow it, because when it calls, the rain will come. On the walls of the Bushmen caves they have depicted the rain bird in many of their art works, as it has a special significance to these people. This symbol is used today by an association trying to bring awareness to the world about the Bushmen plight. They are in danger of extinction due to being hunted by many different ethnic groups, Europeans included. Governments over time haven't been sympathetic to one of the oldest people on the face of the earth either. I have never met a happier, nor more spiritual people in my life and I have the rain bird tattooed on my arm in their honour.

### I Become a Crocodile Hunter

I want to stress that I am a total animal lover and vegetarian, but when I was a little girl in the bush I was surrounded by cruelty. Nature itself is cruel; it has to be, so that everything can survive, everything is eating everything else. I have never liked hunting and trapping and unfortunately things have got out of hand where these things are concerned, with big money at stake. There wasn't much talk of illegal hunting in those days, but I know that hunting crocodiles and smuggling the skins out of the country was taboo. There was a crocodile hunting gang in the Kasane area that my Dad and the local police were trying to catch, but to no avail. They knew that it was going on and they knew it was under their noses and that the skins were leaving the country, but nothing more.

There was a white man that I called Uncle Keith who lived not too far from us along the river. He was in charge of a company that recruited African men for the mines in South Africa. Uncle Keith was a sturdy, dark-eyed, leather-skinned South African, always dressed in khaki. He always wore his old felt hat that had a ring of crocodile teeth around the crown. A lot of men wore this bush uniform, and they all had teeth, claws, feathers or whatever trophies they had shot on them, a sign of primitive prowess and very macho. Uncle Keith would sometimes come to dinner, or we would go to his house for a meal, which was always cooked by a cook boy. He wasn't married at that time, but wanted a wife. There were a lot of single men wanting to get married, but there were no young ladies around and nowhere to meet them and if they did meet them, not many women wanted the sort of life that these men had to offer, it was too isolated and lonely. Many men went to South Africa, Rhodesia or England looking for a bride and some of them came out to the bush with these poor vulnerable women who hadn't a clue what awaited them. Many of these marriages ended before they even had a chance to start. Uncle Keith was always on the lookout.

One day, out of boredom, I walked along the river bank until I got to Uncle Keith's place. I wasn't planning on going there at all. I was just rambling along under a very hot sky, singing to myself. Suddenly I heard Uncle Keith's voice, he was ranting and raving and swearing, "you bloody kaffirs, you are ruining the bloody skins, they won't be any good by the time you've finished skinning them, get off for Christ's sake". Now at the age of nearly four, I could swear with the best of them, especially in Setswana, but I never liked the K word and the way it was said and I didn't like using Christ's name in vain either, because Aggie told me it was a sin, although Mum and Dad seemed to think it was alright because they used it often enough, as did everyone else around me. Uncle Keith wasn't happy to see me.

"Ag man, the bloody DC's daughter, this is all I need now to fuck things up".

"Hello Uncle Keith," said I, as I approached the clearing under the mopane trees. Under the trees lay about six big dead crocodiles. In the centre of the clearing there was a crocodile lying on its back with its soft white belly exposed, with a bloody gash in the throat. Sitting astride the animal was the biggest black man I had ever seen, he was enormous, with huge powerful arms and thighs, dressed only in a pair of ragged shorts. The colour of this man's skin was blue-black and it was shiny with crocodile blood. His big feet, on each side of the crocodile were digging into the sand, trying to anchor himself while he sat on the crocodile with a big *panga* in his two hands. The knife was deep inside the croc's throat and he was pulling it down to slit the soft under-belly of the animal. There was a man on either side of the crocodile waiting for this blue-black fellow to finish slitting the skin from throat to tail and then their job was to each pull at the skin from each side and then finish skinning the crocodile completely, releasing a perfect whole skin. I had walked into something that I wasn't supposed to see.

Uncle Keith turned his attention to the men again and told them that they were too heavy to sit on the soft skin of the crocodile's belly and that they were destroying the skins. The trouble was that all the men were enormous and heavy. The men stood around looking sheepish and grumbling among themselves, while Uncle Keith walked towards me. His eyes studied me carefully and I was a little nervous because I thought he was cross with me.

"Do you like secrets Susy?" and I nodded yes, "and do you like sweeties?" and I nodded again. So that was how uncle Keith employed me and I became part of the crocodile smuggling ring that my Dad was after and all at the age of not quite four. I was only dressed in my panties and was bare foot as always.

Uncle Keith showed me what I had to do and gave me the knife. I had to straddle the crocodile and do what the African had done, cut from the throat downwards and as I cut, I slid backwards towards the tail. As I cut, a man each side would pull at the skin so that it came away from the body. I was light so I didn't ruin the skin. I did this with every crocodile lined up under the trees for skinning. The knife was extremely sharp and when I think of anyone in their right sense letting a small child handle a weapon like that, I cringe and I wouldn't think of letting my kids handle a knife like that, but times were different then and circumstances were different, right or wrong. The whole scene was bizarre. When I had finished my job, an African washed me down with a hose to get rid of all the slime and blood and then I lay in the sun to dry off. Uncle Keith came and sat next to me after plying me with coolie sweeties that were bright pink, very hard, very old and full of the inevitable gritty dust and I loved them. He told me that I had done a really good job and that I could come back every day if I wanted to, but I wasn't to tell my daddy or anyone else, otherwise there would be no more sweeties, so I did go back and I didn't tell Dad or anyone else. The next day after skinning, Uncle Keith let me salt the skins with the Africans. We would go down on our hands and knees and rub salt into the skins, and get them ready for drying. When the skins were dry and ready for shipping out of the country, they were put into mokoros and we would go up the river and bury the skins in the vertical sides of the river bank and cover up any evidence by smearing mud over the entrance so that nobody could see that anyone but the kingfishers had made their nests there.

I would go with Dad and his policemen in their motor boat during the day, looking for evidence of crocodile hunters. We would go up and down the river, stopping every now and then to dig and scratch around looking for clues, but nothing was found and I kept quiet because I was onto a good thing here.

At night Uncle Keith would remove the skins and take them up river into Rhodesia where he would sell them.

This gambit went on all the time I was in Kasane and when we left I thought I would never see Uncle Keith again, but I did, twenty two years later in South Africa.

I was sitting at the cot-side of my second baby, in a hospital in Johannesburg. My little boy was only a couple of months old and was very ill with pneumonia. My husband and I took turns to be by his bedside, because my husband had to work. There were other mothers in the brightly painted ward, all vigilant of their sick children. In the bed next to my son was a little blonde, deeply tanned girl of about eight, who was in for measles complications. Her mother was a very tall gangly woman, with a very bad haircut, as if cut with a nail scissors. We exchanged pleasantries and asked about each other's children and their illnesses, but no more. Then one afternoon, a crocodile Dundee look-alike walked into the ward and I felt my mouth fall open as I stared at this dusty, khaki man. He walked over to the bed next to ours and kissed the little girl and the woman and asked in a strong South African accent if she was feeling better. I watched this scene closely and knew without a doubt that it was Uncle Keith and yet I couldn't believe it. We had lost touch with him when we left Kasane and I was just a little tot.

"What are you looking at lady? Don't you know it's rude to stare?". This was directed at me who was still gaping like an idiot.

"Is your name Keith?" I asked,

"So what if I am? What's it to you?" he replied, looking very suspicious by now and so was his wife by this time, who was glaring daggers at me.

"Uncle Keith, you don't remember me do you?"

"No, should I?"

Then I jogged his memory, about way back, when I was part of his gang. He grabbed me and swung me around in the air as if I was still that little girl of four, tears streaming down his cheeks and laughing at the same time. He told his wife who I was and she softened a bit. We had a lovely long chat about those days and I told him what I had done with my life since then and he told me what he had done with his. He had found the wife he was seeking and had four children. Although he had aged, he had done it well and was still living in the same area and was still doing the same things. His little girl was discharged that same afternoon and they were going back to Botswana, as it was called by then. When he gave me a big farewell hug, he looked into my eyes and said, "you never did tell your Dad, did you? I knew I could bank on you my girl".

No I never did tell my Dad, at least not until last year, with me a fifty-four year old woman and Dad in his eighties, fifty years later.

I live in Spain now with my Spanish husband and I brought my Dad out from South Africa for my eldest son's wedding and one day we were sitting over a glass of red wine reminiscing about the past. He loved talking about those days in the bush and all the characters we came into contact with. He started on the crocodile smugglers story.

"Suzy, do you remember when you came with us in the motor-boat, up and down the river, looking for clues? Such a bloody shame I didn't catch the buggers".

I decided to put an end to the story and tell him all about my part in the crime. It took the best part of that sultry Spanish afternoon and another bottle of wine, to tell Dad all about it. He was absolutely flabbergasted. "And I didn't know a thing", he said.

"No Dad, you never knew a thing about what I did, where I was, how I felt, nothing."

Dad and I had lived in the same house, but each of us lived in a different Africa and saw things with different eyes, it's just the way things were in colonial Africa. I sometimes feel that the offspring of the colonialists were the "other" victims of colonialism. We were brought up by African servants and when old enough, at about five or six, as in my case, shipped off to boarding school. We changed homes and schools continuously, never gelling in one place, never in one place long enough to make or keep friends. We were a very lonely bunch of kids and many grew up having real problems. I cannot deny that my experiences were something that many people envy and I am lucky to have had them, but I think one has to weigh up the pros and cons carefully before judging. I blamed my parents for years at the choices they made to satisfy themselves, without taking us children into consideration, but I have come to terms with it now and realise that my father went through the same thing himself when he was a child, with his parents, so it is just passed on down the line.

I do have to say, that I have great respect for crocodiles and I have asked forgiveness from them, hoping that their spirits will hear me and pardon me, for what I did as an ignorant little girl, who knew no better. Today I cannot condone any hunting whatsoever, unless it's for survival. My contact with crocodile hunters continued in Maun and I will tell you all about that when we get to that chapter.

*Health Issues ~ The Gory Bits!*

Living in the bush one is very vulnerable. Although we had all the inoculations stipulated by the government and were a bright saffron from all the malarial medicine we took, there were so many things that could bite and sting and insects, plants and animals that could maim or kill you, not to mention the very bush itself, that could swallow you up, or the river that could pull you down. The sun was a constant enemy, as was the rain and lightning when it came. Driving anywhere was a hazard because you could get lost, or stuck, as there were no proper roads in those days. And then there were the witch doctors that could put spells on you, poison you, or even kidnap you and turn you into magic *muti* that was very powerful and very expensive. That was a fate that nearly befell me, but that was when we lived in Maun and I will tell you that in the next chapter. Here I am just going to mention some of the illnesses that we came across and how we coped with them.

### Dad

He really only suffered from horrible boils on his backside which were not very exciting, although terribly painful and even more embarrassing because he couldn't sit down and the servants had a royal time laughing at his expense. Mum would put poultices on them until they burst. We had a doctor in Lobatsi and in Maun and Molepolole there were small hospitals, but in Kasane, Rhodesia was our closest and that was hours away and driving through the bush it took ages. We relied on Mum, Duncan and Aggie in any emergency. In Machaneng we had to go into Gaberone.

### Tommy

My little brother who was seven years younger than me, was always falling down and hurting himself, but he was always patched up and sent out to play again. He was a tough little guy, always full of scars, cuts and bruises. He was a very blonde little boy with bright blue eyes and he would suffer terrible nose bleeds from being in the sun. When he was about three he cut himself on the forehead, not a big cut, just a little scratch, but through that he got a streptococcus infection that got out of hand and he was unconscious for a long time. I do not remember for how long, but it seemed to last forever. He was burning with a continuous fever and wasn't aware of anything, which was probably for the best. Mum and Aggie did the best they could while Dad tried to get hold of a doctor, any doctor, in any part of the B.P., but all the doctors seemed to be away on emergencies in far-flung places. Eventually we got a message to a doctor via the radio and he said he was on his way and would be with us as soon as possible, which could be any time at all, with all the things that could go wrong in the bush. The day after Dad had made contact with the doctor, Tom woke up. He shared a bedroom with me because the house didn't have more than two bedrooms. I had pushed our beds together because I wanted to be close to my little brother whom I doted on and I'd hold his sweaty little hand in mine all through every night that he was ill. It was early in the morning before anyone was up and I was lying in bed awake, listening to the stirrings of the birds outside in the dark. I still had Tom's tiny hand in mine, but this morning it felt cooler than it usually felt and I turned to look at him and found his big blue eyes gazing at me, bewildered, as though he was trying to figure out where he had been, or where he was at the moment. "Hello Suzy", he said giving me a big smile. I leaped out of bed and ran to Mum's bedroom, saying that Tom was awake. By the time Mum and Dad had got out of bed and came into our room to see for themselves, Tom was up and running around as though nothing had happened and was no worse for wear. We were delighted of course, but couldn't understand it all and nor could the doctor who had come from afar, just to find his patient who was supposed to be an urgent case, running around like a banshee. Mum invited the doctor to stay for lunch and Dad plied him with enough brandy to placate him.

When Tommy was just a baby, a few months old, he awoke screaming blue murder one morning. It was the height of a very hot summer and Tom was put to sleep in his cot just wearing a terry- towelling nappy, (disposables weren't around in those days). Mum rushed into the bedroom and found him bright red and sweating profusely. When she picked him up he screamed even louder and thinking that the nappy pin had come undone and was sticking into him, she pulled the nappy down over his little bottom. His right buttock was so swollen and inflamed and when she touched it Tom went beserk. She shook the nappy out and out fell an enormous yellow scorpion. Tom was rushed to the little local hospital in Maun and he was treated as best as possible, not knowing what the outcome would be for such a small baby. Tom was a survivor because he overcame that incident too and I am glad to say that he is still around today, after many more mishaps in his life, as a man and as a hunter in the bush, with many tales of his own, to tell his own son one day.

### Mum

When we were living in Kasane Mum had an acute attack of appendicitis. At first she wasn't sure what was causing her stomach ache, but as it got worse, being a nurse, she suspected the worst, so decided to go to the dispensary next door and get Duncan to give his opinion. After examining her he said that they should get her to the hospital in Rhodesia as soon as possible. Dad and Uncle Keith bundled Mum and I into a motor-boat and we were to be met at the border by a car who would take us the rest of the way to the hospital. It was getting dark when we started out on our trip and the hippos were sticking their heads out of the water to look at us as we passed. Our boat's engined died on us and left us in the middle of the river, adrift with the hippos coming dangerously close, rocking the boat. Dad was trying to calm Mum down as she was by now in agony with the pain in her side and Uncle Keith started rowing with the oars that were in the boat. To top it all, we were heading for some rapids which could suck us up and spits us out like the pips of an orange. Thank goodness Uncle Keith knew these waters like the back of his hand, but he had always had a motor before and this was an entirely different kettle of fish. Through sheer hard work, grit and sweat, Uncle Keith got us to the meeting point where a car and driver was waiting for us. We sped into the night and into Rhodesia at the fastest speed the roads would allow us and eventually after what seemed a very long scary night, we deposited Mum in the hospital where they operated straight away. The doctor said that the appendix had burst just as they opened her up. She was very lucky that time.

While in the B.P. Mum became pregnant but lost the baby girl she was expecting in the early months of pregnancy. Not long afterwards, she fell pregnant again, this time with my brother Tom. We were all looking forward to the new baby. We were living in Maun at the time, so we weren't too isolated. There was a women's club called the hens club, which consisted of a large group of white women. They organized fetes and parties and all sorts of cultural, fun and sporting events, mainly to stop the boredom that could overcome white women living in the bush. You had to remember that they all had servants and not just one maid. At one time we had, a maid for the children, a wash- girl who took care of the laundry, a cleaning- girl, who cleaned, a cleaning-boy, who did all the heavy- duty cleaning that the cleaning-girl couldn't do, e.g. windows, polishing the floors and anything else that needed doing. A cook- boy or girl, a gardener, or two and then there were the prisoners who helped do any extras like tree felling, painting etc. And then we had Aggie on top of it all and she was our personal assistant, waitress, manager, housekeeper, personal nanny and general organiser of everybody. Note that I use the term "girl" and "boy", because that is what they were called, regardless of the age of the person and it is a term that rankled with me as a child. I could never understand why a white person of the same age as the black people that we called, "boy" and "girl", we had to call man or woman. Some of the servants were positively elderly and still they were referred to as, "boy" or "girl", it didn't make any sense to me and whenever I asked an adult why this was, they would pat me on the head and tell me to stop asking so many silly questions and to run along and play. But at the age of six or seven, you don't have a say in the matter. So to stop the boredom of everyday life, the white ladies organised whist drives, bingo, bioscope, etc. Whenever one of the ladies in the village was pregnant, like Mum was at the time, the members of the hen club would all give their maternity dresses to the Mum in waiting and they would all do the necessary alterations to fit the new Mum. When she had had her baby the clothes would go back to their rightful owners until the next one needed them. It was a good system with there not being any shops around selling maternity wear.

It must have been about six weeks before the baby was due, not long before Christmas and we were invited to some friends for lunch. I can still remember what Mum wore that day; it was a light-weight linen summer, two-piece suit in navy blue, with a white collar. She was heavy on her feet and enormous and also suffering terribly with the excessive heat. After lunch she got up to go to the outside loo. A lot of houses still only had outside loos and you had to look and make sure before you sat down, that there wasn't a snake curled up behind the toilet, as often happened because they liked the cool dark places. This loo was dark and dank and to get up onto the big wooden seat you first had to climb up onto a pedestal where the toilet was situated. The toilet itself was like a box with a big hole in the middle and everything you did in it went straight into the ground. I went with Mum to the loo because I also needed to go and I was too scared to go on my own. On stepping down off the pedestal, Mum slipped and fell, breaking her leg. She screamed and I screamed and everyone came out of the house to see what had happened. Mum was taken to the hospital and her leg was put into a cast. With her big tummy and leg in plaster she couldn't move and had to sit the rest of her pregnancy out, just waiting.

The baby was late, very late and the doctor was worried and Mum was still in plaster. It was decided to give her a caesarean, so into hospital she went.

They put Mum on the operating table and gave her the anaesthetic. She was so exhausted that she fell asleep. They started cutting, an old fashioned cut, right up the middle of her tummy, when she woke up and said to the doctor, "I can feel everything you are doing". The doctor was flabbergasted, gave Mum a painkiller jab, took the baby out and sewed Mum up as quickly as possible. Just as he had finished sewing, the table collapsed and Mum fell onto the floor, on top of the doctor, with the table on top of them, total chaos and all Mum's stitches had burst. She was sewn up again, but with so much air in her, they threatened to burst more than once. The anaesthetic was out of date and they didn't know and they didn't have any more. Poor Mum was still in plaster too. While she was recuperating in the ward she wasn't allowed to drink anything fizzy in case the stitches burst, doctor's orders. One day a friend of ours, Kenny, the village wide-boy, sneaked into the ward through the window, so that the lion of a matron, a big black mama with attitude, wouldn't catch him. He brought with him an iced cold beer. The temperatures were soaring that summer and Mum was very thirsty, so she gulped the beer down. Needless to say, she had to have more stitches and Kenny was banned from the hospital. She was lucky that she had a pain threshold that was in her favour, she never felt the same degree of pain as other people, but she said that she had never felt pain like that in her life, but she survived and the baby was beautiful.

Aggie took over caring for Mum and the baby who she called, "my little tea-pot". Aggie became a familiar sight in the village, with this very blonde baby asleep tied to her back. She would show off her baby to all and sundry. Mum slowly recovered, although the scar on her tummy was an eyesore until the day she died.

When little Tommy started to get his teeth he became very miserable, as babies often do while teething. Aggie would tie a big piece of dried kudu biltong around his neck on a ribbon and he would sit on a blanket under the marula tree in the garden for hours, just chewing on his salty biltong stick, until it was a sinewy, sticky stump, as happy as can be. When the biltong finished, it was promptly replaced by another stick, anything for peace and quiet. I don't know whether raw dried meat, would meet with Dr Spock's approval, but it worked for Tommy and for Mum.

Mum, Dad and later on, my brother, all got malaria, but I was either luckier or tougher, because I never had it, but I got other ailments, nothing too serious though.

## Me

I had the usual childhood ailments and managed to get through them as any healthy child does. I have already mentioned my adventure during my measles when we lived in Lobatsi. German measles I got when I was older, while living for a while in England after leaving the B.P., after independence and it was nothing to write home about.

While still in Lobatsi, I broke my nose. We were watching a local cricket match from the front of our truck, because it was raining and too wet to sit outside. Dad decided to get closer to the game and drove straight into a donga and I hit my nose on the dash board of the truck. My nose bled profusely and my eyes went black. I was rushed to our neighbour Doctor who said, apart from a pain killer, the only remedy was ice, which I hated. I had to have these ice-packs on my nose four times a day and I would hide in the bush to avoid it, which caused Aggie to swear in every language and dialect she knew. In Lobatsi I also managed to take an overdose of Benson's liver pills. He had left the little bottle of brown pills on the kitchen table and being bored one afternoon while Mum was having a nap, I went into the kitchen looking for sweeties, when I saw what looked like chocolate covered raisins, so I emptied the whole bottle into my mouth and swallowed. Under the coating, these pills were a deep blue and when I started spewing blue out of my mouth, I ran into Mum's room, she picked me up and ran next door with me, where I was given a stomach pump. Benson got a right telling off too.

In Kasane we had what was called a rubber hedge, which was a dark green rubbery plant with long thin leaves that looked like green beans. If you snapped these leaves in half, a thick, sticky, white milk oozed out and if you got this milky substance in your eyes, you could go blind and very quickly too. This shrubby hedge grew everywhere. I loved to snap the leaves and one day I got a fair amount of this milk in my eyes. I can't remember how I did it, whether I rubbed my eyes with my fingers that were full of the stuff, or maybe just tried to see what would happen if I put it directly in my eyes, I do not know, but I remember the drama of it all. If I was told not to do something, I would usually do it, just to see if it would really happen, or to see if I would go to hell, as Aggie would say. Being the staunch catholic that she was, she loved hell fire and brimstone and would try frightening me with all sorts of tortures that awaited me for being a naughty little girl. As soon as this sticky stuff got into my eyes, I started screaming and I could hardly see anything at all. Aggie who had been at the window, saw me and rushed out of the house. On hearing Aggie's screams, Mum also came out and Aggie pushed her out of the way and carried me indoors where she spat in my eyes. Mum winced at this but one look at Aggie's face told her it was wiser to shut up. Aggie then got a jug of milk and while holding me over the basin she poured milk into my eyes continuously for the next hour. As there was no fresh milk available in Kasane, we had to make up jugs of tinned powdered milk and Mum was told to keep mixing jugs up because we were going to need a lot of milk, if I had a chance of maintaining my sight at all. Aggie then put me in my dark bedroom with an ice pack over my eyes and I was told to sleep. When I woke up a couple of hours later, my eyes felt as though they had been boiled and they were very inflamed, but I could see, thanks to Aggie. I am not sure whether it was her spit that did the trick, or whether it was Nestles tinned, powdered milk, but something worked.

I had two nasty bouts of tick bite fever which made me very ill indeed. I also had a lot of fever blisters that were so big that I couldn't eat and had to drink with a straw. I was even off school with them because they would give me terrible fevers and I have suffered with them since then. I had sunstroke a couple of times too, because I was outside under that fierce sun all day without a hat. Nobody told me that I shouldn't do it, so I stayed out until I felt ill and then had to go to bed and be bathed in cold water an vinegar. There was a nasty fly that used to lay its eggs under your skin when you weren't aware of it and then these things would grow until they popped out, or were removed by the doctor. The flies would hide in the washing hanging outside and then when you wore the clothes they would do their evil act. I was always having these little devils removed from different parts of my body.

I got chicken pox while I was at my first boarding school, in a little village called Francistown, at the tender age of six. I had spent the weekend with a school friend who had taken me home with her because it was a long weekend and my parents lived too far to collect me just for three days. I didn't feel too well that weekend and by the time I got back to the school I was running a high temperature and had a nasty rash all over me. The matron put me in the sick bay which was at the far end of the boarding facilities and told me that I was in quarantine so that I wouldn't infect the other children. I had terrible nose bleeds with the chicken pox and I had to cope on my own. I was left in this room alone for two weeks without anyone coming to see me, not even the doctor or the matron. The African maid would leave trays of food outside the door and when I had finished my meals I would have to put the tray outside again. I remember that Dad just happened to be in Francistown for a business meeting, so he came to see me. He stayed for five minutes and left me a stick of biltong and said goodbye. I remember crying a lot at that time, because I felt sick, afraid and terribly lonely. When I look back, I now know that it wasn't the way to treat a little girl of six, but at the time I just got on with it. The matron's Alsatian came in to visit me every day and when Dad left that day, I gave the dog my biltong.

### Others

A lot of people had malaria, but as I mentioned before, I was lucky to escape it. Quite a few people died of bilharzia, which one got from contact with infected water. In the rivers there were leeches too, big black slimy things that would stick all over us when we went swimming. Tsetse fly was rife and our vehicles had to go through dips of disinfectant when we went from one area to another, so that we wouldn't take the disease with us on our tyres. Animals were also dipped. Tsetse causes sleeping sickness.

There were all sorts of diseases, plants, viruses, insects and animals that could maim or kill you in Africa, so one was always on the lookout and always being warned, but none of these things affected me. I felt that I belonged and that I was in my natural habitat.

We had a friend who only had one arm because his other arm had been bitten off by a lion. I would stare at him for ages, fascinated by the empty sleeve of his safari suit. He was a professional hunter, so it was all part of the game as far as he was concerned and even with only one arm, he still went hunting. We heard of many lion attacks, just as we heard of many, leopard, warthog, hippo, crocodile, snake and other animal attacks on humans who went where they shouldn't have gone, encroaching into the animals comfort zone. We had a neighbour in Maun, who kept baboons in a huge cage that ran the whole length of her garden. We used to stop by on the way back from school and watch her feed them. She used to take huge bowls of mixed fruit and vegetables into the cage, singing as she went in, "who's got some yummy foodies for her babies?" and the baboons would go berserk and start barking until she left the cage and then they would devour all the food, stuffing it into their mouths in a feeding frenzy. One day we went by her house and the baboons were gone, so we knocked on her door to ask her what had happened to the monkeys, but she wasn't there either. It turned out that the day before, she had gone in to feed the apes, just like she did every day, but when she turned around to leave the cage, the baboons attacked and killed her and not being satisfied with what they had done, they ate her too, every bit of her, leaving just the bones. The police had come and shot the baboons and her house went up for sale.

Most people had anti snakebite kits at home, at least we were advised to have the serum, just in case. Those who didn't have a kit, were those folk that thought, it would never happen to them. We knew a man with only one hand and he told us how he lost it. He had gone to his only neighbour for supper one night. This neighbour lived a fair way from his house and he decided the walk there would do him good, as it was such a nice evening. To get to his friend's house he had to walk through the bush, but as the sun was just setting and it was still light, he didn't mind. He hadn't thought about walking back in the dark after supper and hadn't even taken a torch with him, which is standard equipment in the bush. He and his friend had a good supper and then started the serious drinking, brandy being the favourite bush tipple. They drank well into the night and by the time this man was ready to head for home, both he and his friend were as pissed as newts. He stumbled out into the pitch black, moonless night and headed for home. Staggering through the bush, he felt something bite his hand. Through his drunken haze, he was convinced that he had been bitten by a snake, so he started running as best as he could in his condition. He stumbled into his kitchen, lit a paraffin lamp, took a meat cleaver out of the drawer and then sat down at the kitchen table, laying his bitten hand on the wooden surface, raised the cleaver and brought it hard down on his wrist, severing his hand completely. By this time he was totally sober. He tied a towel around his arm as tightly as possible and took the hand with him to the dispensary where they patched him up and then sent him to the nearest hospital. It turned out that he wasn't bitten by a snake at all, but was pierced by a long thorn which was still embedded in his severed hand. He thought that if he cut his hand off before the snake poison got any further into his system, he would survive.

There was also rabies around and with a lot of stray dogs roaming the streets and the bush, it was a worry for all of us, especially as we all had pets that were free to wander where they wanted to. When we lived in Maun we had friends whose spaniel got rabies. They were a really nice Dutch family, he was the weather man in Maun and his wife did a lot of baking and sewing for the community. They had two very blonde children, who although were a bit younger than me, I used to play with them. Their dog was still a puppy and I don't remember whether it had been vaccinated against rabies yet or not. One day it started foaming at the mouth and went absolutely berserk, so they locked it up in the bedroom and called the vet and the police, who shot it through the window. Although the children hadn't been bitten, they had been playing with the dog who had licked them. The treatment they had to undergo at that time, was an injection in their stomachs with a very large needle, every day for fourteen days. These poor little mites were desperate with fear and would run to my house where I would hide them under my bed. But we were always found out and Mum explained that if they didn't have the dreaded injections they could die. I felt like a traitor to them when I handed them over to their mother for the injections. Nevertheless, they survived and they forgave me too which was so important to me. I think treatment today has advanced somewhat.

I consider myself lucky as far as safety was concerned, because there were dangers around every corner and I managed to avoid the worst of them. I guess I had a very caring angel watching over me at all times.

# 5.   Maun

So here we were in another town, in another house, after another three months leave in the UK. When we got to Maun, our ever faithful Aggie was there waiting for us, ready to get our new home in order.

Maun was a big bush town with a lot more white people and a few more African and Indian shops, so we didn't feel so isolated. Our house was much bigger than we had had before too and the garden was enormous, with a beautiful big flame tree in the back yard that we made a tree house in. At the back of the house, there were the usual servants' quarters, the big boiler that was kept lit to give us hot water, roast mopane worms and dispose of snakes in. There was also a very big area that was called the wood pile, which was just that, a very big clearing where we would get our wood delivered for the boiler. The woodpile was shaded by big pepper-corn trees and it was where the gardener would chop the wood into blocks, for feeding the ever burning boiler. It was also a place I liked to play, or just to sit on the big felled tree trunks in the shade and smell the clean wood shavings and the peppery scent of the peppercorns above, as they rustled in the breeze. In the front of the house we even had a swimming pool. It wasn't a beautiful big blue pool, but a small, deep, square, grey concrete pool, that always seemed to be filled with a green slimy water, that we shared with frogs and lots of other creepy crawlies. But we loved our pool. There was the typical veranda that ran all around the house, the mosquito netting and the scrubby yellow lawn in the front, were the norm in all of our houses. The whole property was surrounded by the standard wire fencing, which we would climb over, to play with the kids next door. At least in Maun I had other friends to play with, which was nice, but also rather daunting, as I had got used to playing by myself. It would also be the place where I went to a proper white school. I will tell you more about all my schools later on in the book.

The best of all, was the fact that we actually had neighbours and a hospital, a hotel and a tennis club. The hen's club organised all sorts of entertainment to fit in and around the town's main past time among the whites, drinking. We also lived right on the river bank which for me was the best thing of all.


## Thruppence

Thruppence was the name of our cook boy, so called, because as he said himself, "I am so small". He was a short little fellow with a permanent smile on his face. He not only cooked, but also polished the floors and helped out with whatever needed doing. He didn't do the garden though, because we had a gardener that did that, together with the prison gang who would come along escorted, to do the heavy stuff. Aggie needed help because this house was much bigger and there was a lot of both, official and non-official entertaining to do.

One day Thruppence came on duty as drunk as a skunk. Mum was furious and told him that he was fired. She wasn't too pleased because she had a big dinner party that evening and had put in a lot of time and trouble getting things ready. Thruppence was to cook the meal, which was to be a roast, potatoes and vegetables, followed by an apple pie and tinned cream. The pie was to have been baked by Thruppence. So it was Mum and Aggie that got together and prepared the meal. They decided that there wasn't time to bake a pie and that they would whip up a packet of chocolate pudding instead.

The long trestle tables were pushed together in the big dining-room and were covered by starched white sheets, which were much bigger than any table cloth that was available and looked just as good. The gleaming silverware and wine glasses were in place and there were beautiful arrangements of bougainvillea and flame flowers along the centre of the table, all from our garden. The guests arrived, cocktails were drunk and then everyone went into dinner. The roast springbok was crisp and tender, the potatoes, just right and even the home grown vegetables raised comments from the distinguished guests. These were official guests, not good friends, but people Mum and Dad had to entertain, government officials, v.i.p.'s.

Mum rang the little table bell when everyone had finished their main course and Aggie came in to remove the plates. She looked at Mum and tried to catch her attention, but Mum was engaged in conversation with one of the guests and didn't pay much attention to her. Everyone carried on drinking their wine and chatting while waiting for their dessert. The door opened and in walked Thruppence, with the biggest pie you can imagine. In the pie was a lit sparkler. He carried this dish into the dining room and put it down in front of Mum. On the top of the pie was written, "I am very sorry madam", in what looked like a golden pastry. He avoided Mum's eyes and left the room. Mum was really angry, because she thought that Thruppence had left that morning as he was told to do. Being the perfect hostess, she proceeded to cut into the pie and dished it up to the guests as if nothing out of the ordinary had happened. She passed the jug of cream around and then cut herself some pie. The pastry looked very fluffy, not like the usual pie crust. She took a mouthful and realised that it was mashed potato on top of the apple filling and not pastry. She apologised to her guests and explained what had happened that morning with Thruppence. Fortunately, everyone thought it was a really funny story and a good topic of conversation for the rest of the evening. Thruppence was saved and in the end he stayed with us for the two years we were in Maun.

## The River

The river was a continuous source of entertainment for us. At night sometimes, friends of Dad's who had a boat, would organise a spearfishing outing. We would take a picnic supper and lots of beers and would go out nearly half the night. It was really exciting and a little scary, being on those murky waters in the dark.

During the day I would often go down to the river by myself, or with a few little friends, to swim and play around in the shallows. I had a mask and snorkel which I loved because the water was so transparent in a lot of places and you could see all sorts of animals under the surface. The bird life was spectacular too. The river was always a hive of activity. The big danger, as always, was the crocodiles and the hippos. If we saw a croc, we got out of the water until it swam past and then we would get back into the water again. I saw a croc take a little black child who was swimming with his friends not far from us. We ran back to tell our parents and the police went in search for the crocodile. They found one with a very fat stomach and shot it. When they opened the animal up, they found the little boy. These attacks were quite common there, because people would do their washing in the river and they would fish too, so there was always the risk.

The policemen in Maun rode horses and when they were off duty they took the horses down to the river and leave them on the banks where the animals would graze on the sweet succulent river grass that was always green and very juicy. One day I also saw a crocodile take one of the horses, while I just sat and watched in horror, there was nothing I could do.

*Sacha*

Sacha and Sidney were a strange couple that we met in Maun. Sidney was British and had met Sacha in China, while he was working in the customs office there,

Sacha came from a poor family in Russia. To help the family, she cleaned the floors of a dance studio after school. One day while she was scrubbing the floors on her hands and knees, Pavlova walked in and started talking to Sacha and she was so impressed with the young girl that she gave her lessons in ballet and although Sacha never became a professional dancer, she danced her way through every day of her life. At fourteen she met a young soldier of fifteen and they got married and had a baby boy. But the Russian revolution came and her young husband was killed in front her and her baby was bayoneted. Sacha escaped to China where she met Sidney, a British customs official working in that country and they got married. But the Chinese uprising came along and once again, Sacha and Sidney left their home, escaping in a little boat. After many adventures and mishaps in their lives, they ended up in the B.P. and we kept in contact with them for many years until they died. Sidney was a quiet, polite man, a real gentleman, whereas his Sacha was a typhoon. She was a very fat woman, with long grey hair down to her knees that she would plait and wind around her head. She wore beautiful coloured dirndl skirts, off the shoulder blouses, a battered straw hat and men's working boots. Everyone loved Sacha and Sacha loved everyone. She could also get into terrible tempers.

One evening Dad was having a drink at the local hotel bar with Sidney and seeing that Sidney had far too much to drink, he decided to take him home to Sacha. Sacha thanked Dad for bringing her Sidka home and said goodnight to him. The next day we were invited to Sacha and Sidney's for Christmas lunch, which I was looking forward to because Sacha was a fantastic cook and did all sorts of exotic dishes. She had promised me that she would make me some home- made mango ice-cream.

When we arrived at their house, Sacha flew out of the door with an enormous carving knife, ranting and raving, that Dad had got her Sidka drunk and that she was going to cut off his willy. We got into our Chev and made a quick exit, so it was farewell to my mango ice-cream. She soon forgot about the incident and everyone knew that she was very volatile. She was always kept at arm's length when in a temper, but was always forgiven when she had calmed down.

Once when we were on a trip into the bush, we came across Sacha marching through the bush in her colourful outfit and carrying a suitcase. We stopped and asked where she was going and why she was so far from home. She said that she was walking to Cape Town to get a ship to England, because she was leaving Sidney. She refused to talk about it anymore and also refused to get a lift with us, so we went on our way. We heard that she made it to Cape town, walking all the way from the B.P. and when she got there, she went and sat on the docks and tried hitch-hiking a mail ship by sticking her thumb out. Obviously this didn't work, so she decided to give Sidney another chance and walked all the way through the bush again, back to her Sidka. That was quite a feat because Sacha wasn't a young woman then. We never knew how old she was, but she was always old.

One day she came to our house in Maun and asked Mum if she could take me fishing with her. Mum said it would be fine, so off we went in Sacha's beat up old truck, just Sacha and me. We got to Matlapaneng Bridge, just on the outskirts of the village and Sacha said we were going to fish from the bridge. She handed me a fishing rod, but she held a rifle. We sat down on the bridge with our legs dangling over the side. It was a hot drowsy afternoon and she told me tales of her past in Russia and China. Suddenly she stopped in mid-sentence and took aim into the water and fired. She pulled me up and dragged me down to the water's edge and between the two of us, we hauled an enormous crocodile out of the water. She had shot the beast between the eyes, a perfect shot. At that precise moment, a truck pulled up under the nearby trees and a white man with a felt hat pulled down over his eyes, dressed in the uniform khaki of hunters, got out. He had a rifle slung over his shoulder, just like Sacha. She told me to stay with the crocodile and she went over to the man. I couldn't hear what they were saying, but I could see her pointing to the crocodile and he handed over a thick wad of notes to her, which she promptly stuffed down her bosom. The man and his black helper, who was sitting in the back of the truck, picked up the crocodile, put it into his truck and they sped off in a cloud of dust. Sacha told me it was time to go home, but I whined that we hadn't caught any fish yet. She soon calmed me down with promises of mango ice-cream, which I instinctively knew I would get this time. I was told never to tell anyone about what had happened and I didn't. It seemed that I was destined to be a crocodile hunter. I was going on for six at that time.

Sacha was always the life and soul of the party. When we left the B.P. after independence, we went back to England, but fate had other ideas and after two years in Newcastle on Tyne, Dad found a job in Sierra Leone and then in Johannesburg. I am just mentioning this in passing, because I just want to finish telling you about Sacha.

Years later Mum was waiting for a bus after shopping in Hillbrow. On the bench at the bus stop, there sat Sacha, now very old and very sad looking. After big hugs and weepy kisses, Sacha told Mum what had happened since they last saw each other all those years ago. Sidney had died and now Sacha was living in a bed sit in Hillbrow. She was very lonely and very poor. Mum took her under her wing and Sacha became a part of our lives again. Eventually the South African authorities decided to deport her to England, simply because she was a Russian and therefore a communist and therefore a threat to the country. So poor Sacha had to leave Africa. She was sent to England because her husband had been an Englishman. The British consulate was very good to her and found her a good home in the UK and she wrote and said that she was happy where she was. Mum and Dad went back to England to live eventually and they made contact with Sacha again. When she died, Sacha left me a pair of earrings and an old silver-backed hairbrush. I had used that hairbrush to brush out her long silver hair, plait it and wind it around her head the way she liked it. And while we had these hair afternoons, we would reminisce about the old B.P. days and her youth in Russia and China and she would shed tears over her long dead baby son. She could never have any more children after the death of her baby. I used to love those sultry intimate afternoons, while she sang old Russian love songs and talked about past days, while I brushed her long, old silver hair. In her will she said that she wanted her ashes scattered on the Thamalakane River in Maun. Mum and Dad never had the opportunity to go back to Maun, so Sacha's ashes sat on Mum and Dad's mantelpiece for a few years. One day a mutual friend came to visit my parents, who at the time, were living in the village of Polesworth, in the Midlands in England. While sitting in front of the fire, conversation got around to the good old days in the B.P. and then Mum told him about Sacha's ashes. It just so happened that this friend, who had also loved Sacha, was going to South Africa the next week in the Concorde and then on to Maun, on a business trip and he offered to take Sacha's ashes and scatter them on the waters of the Thamalakane. So that is the end of my story about one of those rare characters that one found in the middle of the bush. She was a dear friend and will never be forgotten.

### Christmas

Christmases in Maun were a lot of fun. Christmas is in summer and very hot, so most of the parties were outside, when the sun went down. About two months before Christmas, the hens club would have a meeting about Christmas. Firstly they would elect four women to go to Johannesburg in South Africa, to do Christmas shopping. Every mother would write a list of gifts and goodies that they wanted and then money would be collected and the four women would go off on a spree.

The big Christmas party would be held either in the local hotel, or in our house and the whole village would come, the whites, that is and there would be presents for everyone and food and drink galore. In the afternoon it would be for the kids and then in the evening it would be for the adults, with a fancy dress ball. The new year's eve dinner dance was also a big do, usually at the hotel, with dancing well into the morning.

The big Christmas tree was usually a big thorn tree, which was ideal because the long white thorns looked like snow and these lethal thorns would keep little fingers and pet's noses well away from the decorations.

Christmas lunch would be a roast, turkey if we could get it, or if not, whatever meat that was hunted. Christmas pudding with a thick brandy sauce, mince pies and Christmas cake, were all dutifully consumed despite the sweltering heat and all this was washed down with a continuous flow of alcohol that had started being drunk at the beginning of December and continued into well after the New Year. People out there always drank a lot, but Christmas was a good excuse to celebrate and it let people feel that they were justified in doing it because it was the festive season. It was typical on Christmas day to start with a breakfast of an enormous mixed grill, washed down with champagne cocktails and black velvets and that was just the start of the day, solidly continuing until 2$^{nd}$ January.

The servants loved Christmas and at the beginning of December the big cleaning would get underway, with all the servants singing carols as they went about their chores. They would all get a Christmas bonus, a food hamper, gifts for all their family, new items of clothing, a bottle or two of liquor and a slap- up Christmas meal. I think all this made up for the fact that they were the ones who had to clean up after the parties that we had and often they would do it in an alcoholic haze, but as everyone else was in the same boat, nobody noticed, except us kids, the only ones not drinking, unless we could slurp up the dregs in the glasses when nobody was looking. Early on Christmas morning, the servants would go around all the houses carol singing, collecting everyone else's maids and garden-boys, cleaners and cooks, so that the group would get bigger as the morning went on. They would sing in Setswana and their voices were those of angels. It brought tears to everyone's eyes to hear them and at the end of the day they had collected quite a sum, which was divided up among them.

My grandparents in England always sent out huge parcels at Christmas time. Our presents were hidden in high-up cupboards that we were supposedly unable to climb, but which we did. There was a lot of foodstuff in those parcels too, things like gentlemen's relish and special marmalade, biscuits and exotic tins, fancy chocolates and stem ginger. There was also crackers from Harrods,( from my snooty gran) and the odd thermal vest,(from my Welsh gran, who didn't really know where in the world Bechuanaland Protectorate was.)

Father Christmas was elected by the hen's club and every year it was a different man. The first year we were there, one of the young English doctor's was chosen and there couldn't have been a character so far removed from the Santa figure, as this poor fellow. He was new in Maun and this was the way the do-good ladies tried to get him to mix with the village. He was a bit of a loner and people thought he was odd because he wore long white robes and walked bare foot. Often you could see him riding a donkey along the banks of the river at sunset. Us kids used to call him Jesus, because of the robes and the donkey. He was very young, very, thin and very bald, so they had their work cut out for them. They padded him out in a sweltering suit and be-furred him in a mountain of cotton wool, not only to give him a big beard but also a long head of fluffy white hair. He was bought up the river in a mokoro and when he got off the craft he was mounted on a donkey that carried him up to the hotel where the party was being held. By the time he got off the donkey, his beard and false hair were dripping with sweat and it didn't help that we chanted Jesus, Jesus, Jesus, as he came up the hotel driveway.

The second year we were in Maun, Dad was to be Santa, which would have been fine, had we not noticed his watch on his wrist and that was a definite deception to me realising that Dad was in fact Father Christmas.

### The Hotel

The one and only hotel in Maun was the watering hole for the white community. All functions, parties and celebrations were held there. It was an old fashioned colonial building with a big veranda around the main building and it had a tin roof. The rooms were behind the building and the gardens were big and shady. There was a swimming pool in the front and next to the hotel was the tennis club, which was handy after a thirsty game. Every Friday night people would congregate in the bar for drinks and us kids were left to our own devices on the veranda. We were given a dragon's blood, which was a virulent red cordial and a big packet of cheese crisps and told to behave ourselves, which we never did.

On Saturday nights there would be movies in the hotel lounge, where a big portable screen on a stand was erected. They were usually Doris Day , or black and white films that us kids couldn't understand very well. The grown-ups sat in chairs at the back of the lounge with their drinks and us kids would sit or lie on the floor in the front, guzzling chocolate bars. The reel nearly always broke down umpteen times during the evening and it would take ages to get it started again. Often we would get bored and slip out into the garden and let all the air out of the car tyres. When it was time to go home all the men had to start pumping air, swearing at the moon above, while we ran around in the dark, whooping with the sheer exuberance of youth, freedom and night air.

The hotel had a big dining room where we went for a meal on special occasions. The tables were covered with stiff, starched, white tablecloths and the chairs were high and heavy, so that when I sat on one, my little legs stuck straight out under the table cloth instead of dangling. The cutlery was big, not only for little hands, but for adults too, enormous silver tools that made eating an adventure. I can remember that there was always a choice of three soups, mushroom, tomato and my favourite, brown Windsor soup, which I would sip off the end of an enormous boat-like spoon, making slurping noises that echoed around the dining room. Mum would tell me off and to behave like a lady, but there was no way I could get that spoon into my mouth to stop the noises. Another favourite of mine was marrowbone on toast. This dish I have never seen anywhere in the world, apart from Africa. A little triangle of toast would be placed in the middle of huge white plate and then on top of the toast was a round marrowbone with the marrow inside, which you had to manoeuvre out of the bone onto the toast. After adding salt and pepper, this delicacy would be gone in a blink, it was so fatty and it dripped down your chin, delicious. There were the usual steaks, curries, fish and chicken dishes and on Sundays the roast dinner. On some occasions there would be a *braaivleis* (barbeque) in the gardens, where a whole ox would be roasted and served with thick wads of mielie pap and sauce.

*Easter*

The hens club would do the same at Easter as they did at Christmas and would go to Johannesburg to buy the Easter eggs and together with what the grannies from England sent out, I did very well by them all. It was not surprising that I was a fat little girl. I loved Easter because everyone in Maun would get together and we would all go and camp at Matlapaneng Bridge. This was a truly lovely place, with a big clearing under lots of big shady trees. The river was as clear as crystal and the riverbank had sand as white as a beach. The men would set up the camp, lots of tents, tables, chairs and a big BBQ. All of us children would sleep in the same big tent, which was half the fun. There was also a lot of coming and going among the grownups at night into various tents, I didn't understand it then, but looking back now, a lot of things make sense now, that didn't then. The women had cooked and baked for weeks ahead of Easter and there was a continuous flow of food throughout the day. We would get up at dawn to watch the animals coming to drink and then we would have breakfast in the blue morning mist, watching the steam from our mugs of tea, rising to mingle with the dew on the mopane leaves above us. The men had erected a tractor tyre swing from a big tree over hanging the river and we would swing from this tyre and jump into the river. The men and the older and braver children would jump from the Matlapaneng Bridge, but that was really high. We all brought our pets with us, so Jaggers was with me. We all brought our servants too, to do the dirty work and to look after the smaller kids so that the parents didn't have to be troubled by them and could get on with the serious business of drinking. Some people would fish and what was caught was put on the braai. We didn't stop all day, playing in the sun, dressed only in our costumes that we didn't change out of for almost a week. We were as brown as nuts and always hungry, which wasn't a problem because there was so much food. One man was always on croc and hippo patrol and when one of these animals were spotted, the alarm went up and we all got out of the water until the beast swam past and then we all got back into the water again. There were so many games that we played and we were never bored. I consider myself very lucky to have been able to play in total freedom. We never had television, video games, computers or any expensive toy. We just invented games and we had the added advantage of nature itself, she is a great playmate. At the Easter camp there were always snakes being killed, but nobody was bitten. There was a snake bite kit and a first aid kit with us at the camp, but it was seldom, if ever used. On Easter Sunday we all had to hunt for our Easter eggs in the bush, which was fun because there were so many hiding places, that it would take all morning to find them all. Sometimes the sun would be so hot and by the time we found some of the eggs, they were a drippy melting mess, but that didn't matter because we would lick the chocolaty mess off the silvery paper while sitting waist deep in the river. We used to eat big juicy orange mangoes like that too, in the river, where we could wash off the juice at the same time. Our mothers had it easy.

*Tom*

As I mentioned earlier in the book, my brother Tom was born in Maun. I told you all about his dramatic arrival in an earlier section of the book, but I just wanted to add a bit more about my little brother, whom Aggie called "teapot". I remember when Dad told me that he had been born and that we were going to the hospital to see him and Mum. Aggie dressed me in a clean pink dress and forced my feet into a pair of sandals. I hated shoes, but in celebration of a new brother I would comply, just this once. We went into the ward and there was Mum propped up with her leg still in plaster and her tummy very bloated under the sheet. I gave her a kiss and looked around me for the baby, but he wasn't anywhere to be seen. I was just about to ask where he was, when a big fat, black nurse with a huge grin on her face and a smart white uniform covering her buxom figure, walked into the room. Clutched to her breast was a tiny, red, bald, ugly little fellow, wrapped up in a blue blanket. He looked like a new born rat and I loved him to bits from that very moment. I was never jealous of Tommy and I bragged about him to anyone who would listen.

Because Mum was so poorly after the terrible birth and her leg still in plaster, Aggie took over, being more mother than ever before. She looked after Mum, washing, feeding and dressing her, she looked after the baby, me and Dad too. We couldn't have done without her.

When Mum recovered, Tom's christening was planned. Grandma from the Isle of Wight, sent a christening gown and the ceremony was to take place in the court house, with a party to celebrate afterwards at our house. I don't remember too much about the christening, except that Tom slept right through it.

Tim's godparents were, a very posh lady in the big house on the corner, as god mother. And the godfather was a Yorkshire man who worked for the public works department. He was a character and the life and soul of any party.

The Greek butcher gave Tim a lion skin for a christening present. This skin still had the whole head intact, with teeth and all and also the claws. It looked fantastic on the floor, but whenever Dad got up to go for a pee in the middle of the night, he would trip over the lion's head and would swear and curse that bloody Greek every time. So that I wouldn't be jealous, I was given a zebra skin, but I preferred the lion, because mine didn't have claws and teeth.

He grew into a lovely little boy, very blonde with blue eyes like Mum. He cut his teeth on a big stick of biltong on a ribbon around his neck. He ate every insect he found on the floor while crawling and he feared nothing. He was an African baby, used to being strapped to Aggie's back while she did the washing by hand, bent over the bathtub. She would scrub at the stubborn stains, jiggling Tom to sleep with the movement of her humping back and her African lullabies, lulled to hot sweaty dreams under an old frayed blanket.

Tom grew up with his own tales of Africa to tell and maybe one day he will. Unlike me, he went back to Botswana as a young man and made a life there for himself as an adult for many years, before leaving again with his own family to settle in America.


## Weddings

While in Maun we were invited to quite a few weddings, most were average, but there were a couple that stick in my memory that I will mention because they were so different to what we had seen before.

One of Dad's duties was to act as justice of the peace, which meant that he could marry people and when did this for the happy couples; we were usually invited to the wedding. There were times when Dad would have preferred to refuse, but felt that he couldn't.


## Afrikaans Wedding

There were quite a few Afrikaans families living in Maun in those days and they had a lot of the small businesses like the local garage whose mechanic could fix any vehicle that came his way. The local hotel, the general store which looked like one of those shops in the old western movies, selling corn, material, sugar, animal feed, hard dusty sweeties, basins, camphor oil and a long list of unimaginable things that people needed in the bush. Other local businessmen consisted of Indians and Greeks and there were a mish-mash of little shops and pondokkies that made up the village commercial center.

There was a very big influential Afrikaans family in Maun when we were there. I say influential because they were one of the oldest white families in the area and they were cattle ranchers, hunters, shop owners and probably had a lot of other interests scattered about in the area too. I went to school with one of the sons from this family and Dad had a close connection with the father of my schoolmate, through legal and business dealings. One of the daughters was to get married and Dad was to officiate at the wedding, so we were invited, as were half the village, an enormous wedding it was. The bride was a big fat blonde girl with ruddy cheeks and she was dressed in so much puffy white lace and satin that she looked like a cream cake. Her groom was also a big fat fellow, dressed in a green suit and red tie and with so much hair oil on his curly fringe that you couldn't tell whether it was sweat or oil, that was running down the poor lad's face. The ceremony went without a hitch and was fairly quick, but the celebrations went on for a couple of days. The party was held at the family home which was on the outskirts of the village. An enormous dais was erected under a thorn tree and on top of this were two thrones swathed in sugar-pink and white tulle, where the happy couple had to sit overlooking the dance-floor. I say dance floor, but really, it was a circular clearing in the dust, where, as the couples shuffled, the dust would rise in clouds, giving the impression that they were dancing in the clouds. The bride's dress was a nice shade of taupe by the end of the first evening and I cannot imagine what it looked like at the end of the second day's celebration because we only stayed for the first day's party. Our English blood wasn't strong enough to go the whole hog, or at least, that was what Dad said. Across the dance clearing there was a whole ox on a spit that went round and round, dripping grease into the sand

and huge steaks were continuously cut from the beast through the evening. There were hundreds of strings of boerewors sausage flung onto another BBQ, together with chops, chicken, venison, pork, goat, lamb, mielies, baked potatoes, peppers and lots of other things in silver foil that left one guessing. There were huge bowls of different salads, different breads, mielie-pap with bowls of different sauces to dip into. The puddings were in a world of their own, there were different trifles, mousses, jellies, fruit salads, pies, cakes galore, of every type under the sun and of course, the wedding cake, that was a huge pink and white concoction that stood seven tiers high. The whole Boer community of women had been cooking, baking, boiling, roasting and mixing, for months in anticipation of this wedding. And everybody did justice to their effort. The Afrikaners are big, sturdy people and they know how to party big, eat big and drink big. The bar was under another thorn tree in the shade to keep the big vats of ice cool. There was every kind of booze one wanted, on tap and no expense was spared.

This family could have had the wedding at the hotel because they were not short of money, but there were so many people invited and they wanted it on their own property, so they had organised it themselves with the help of their community. The music was generally boeremusiek, which is played on an accordion and to dance to it you pump your arms up and down as you dance around the floor. As I was a child at this wedding, I thought I was in heaven because everyone was so friendly, as the Afrikaners are, especially to children. All the *tannies* (these are the mamas), plied me with so much cake and there was a non-stop flow of cool drink, that I ate and drank till I was sick in the flower beds. I remember going to the veranda of the homestead to take a peep at old Tannie Rosie. Tannie Rosie was the matriarch of this family and everyone was afraid of her. She was very fat, like most of the family and she dressed in a long black dress, tight at the wrists and the neck, so as not to show any flesh. She wore boots with little buttons up the sides and her white hair was always in a tightly drawn back bun at the nape of her neck. Rosie sat in an old rocking chair on that veranda with a stone jug of whiskey on one side of her and a sawn-off shotgun across her lap, together with her bible. We only ever saw her in that position, she never moved from there. She also never spoke to anyone, she didn't like anyone. Whenever the children came and tried to tease her to get a reaction from her, she would fire that shotgun after them, always missing, whether on purpose, or by fluke, we never knew. The night of the wedding, I remember creeping onto the veranda and then Tannie Rosie looked straight at me, aimed her gun and fired. I fell off the edge of the wooden deck, into the gladioli bed below the veranda, safe, but bruised. I ran to tell Mum and Dad, but they patted my arm and said, "yes dear, it's alright, now go and play", so I did.

*Coloured Wedding*

There was a coloured location just outside Maun where Dad's driver lived. This man's daughter was to be wed by Dad, so once again we were invited. This was a totally different affair. The family were holding the party at their home which was a very humble abode. The bride and groom also wore home-made clothes, the groom a badly fitting suit, which swamped his thin frame and made him look so vulnerable. The bride wore a frothy white dress with a long train, which collected dust, chicken shit, toffee papers and everything else that got in the way of her entrance into the house, where the party was held.

I remember getting out of our Chev truck dressed up in a yellow dress with rows of little red clad soldiers, with black busbies on their heads, which had been sewn by the mother of the bride, who was a dressmaker. It was a very hot thundery afternoon with rolling purple clouds overhead. While the ceremony was taking place everyone prayed that it wouldn't rain until after the reception and I think it was the first time I had heard people praying for it not to rain, instead of for it to rain. Rain would have been a disaster for this humble and good-hearted family, because the little house was so small and they were planning to have all the guests outside in the little yard. All the camp chairs they could borrow were already set out in the yard and if the rain had come down, the dusty yard would have been awash with mud and with nowhere to put all the guests. The guests were a mixture of black, coloured and white people and apart from their family, they had invited people who they were grateful to, or were close to in a working environment. The little shack-like house and yard were decorated with party streamers in bright colours and there were bunches of multi-coloured balloons hung over all the doorways in the house. Both inside and out under the Syringa tree, there were trestle tables covered with bright holly-sprigged tablecloths and then laden down with cakes, pies, huge doorstep sandwiches with fillings of margarine and polony, sandwich spread and ham and cheese. There were a lot of angel delight puddings of various colours, sprinkled with hundreds and thousands. We were made welcome and told to take a seat. Then they asked Dad what he would like to drink and he promptly asked for a gin and tonic. That was a big mistake, because these people were very religious and didn't drink at all. They were very proud of the fact that they had a big choice of soft drinks, which included, Canada dry, home brewed ginger beer, ginger ale, cream soda, tonic, soda, coke, Fanta orange, Fanta lemon, Pepsi, cherryade, jugs of made up tang in different shades and a long list of different and brightly coloured cordials. There were also great flowered teapots of tea and coffee on offer. So as you can see, with so much offered, it didn't go down too well when Dad asked for a "proper" drink. I could see straight away, just by looking at my parents, that with a lukewarm glass of pop in one hand and a great big polony doorstep in the other, that our exit would be sooner, rather than later. The wedding cake took pride of place on the table and it was made by one of the family. It was a very tall cake with swathes of white and pink icing to match everything else in the house, but we didn't stay long enough to try it because Dad suddenly remembered a meeting he had to go to, which was with a cold gin and tonic with lots of ice, back home. That wedding was rather like a children's birthday party and being a child I thought it was lovely and was very sad to have been carted away so soon after arrival. Just after we left this friendly humble family, the skies opened and it poured with rain, but I don't know what happened to the wedding party in all that mud. Dad went speeding away as fast as he could. There were urgent matters to see to.

*Indian Wedding*

Although Dad wasn't asked to officiate at Indian weddings because they had their own ceremonies according to their own faiths, either Hindu or Muslim, but he was invited to these weddings sometimes. He didn't go to very many of them, but there was one that Mum and he went to. I was left at home with Aggie on that occasion.

This was an arranged wedding between an older man, a shop keeper of considerable wealth and a young girl of about twelve. The young girl was slim and very beautiful, with long raven hair right down her back. Although I wasn't at the wedding, Dad told me about it years later and I had seen the young girl about town. The wedding was all luxury with no expense spared. There was a lot of silk, gold, jewels and a feast fit for a king. Dad said that the bride was very demur and sat the whole day on a throne with eyes down, not saying a word, while her fat old husband ate, drank, joked and danced the night away, sweating into his big black moustache.

This young girl was soon pregnant and seem to have one baby after another, always being pregnant and soon she looked very haggard and ill. A few years after that wedding, the young woman's family brought their daughter's husband to court for ill-treating her and beating her up so that she was always bruised. He was heavily fined and had to compensate his wife and divorce was granted, so the young girl, who was about fifteen at this time, with a couple children, went back to her family, safe at last, but in disgrace.

## Greek Wedding

There were a lot of Greeks living in Maun, as there were in a lot of areas in the B.P. This story was told to us by a friend who had lived in Maun for many years and it happened just before we lived there.

There was a Greek trader who had a general store, similar to the ones I mentioned earlier. He was in his forties, single and very fat and ugly. He wanted a wife, but there was no chance of that, living in the bush. One night he was having a drink with his best friend, another Greek and moaned about the fact that he was getting old and how he wanted a wife and children. His friend suggested that he send a photo of himself and write to the family in Greece and ask them to send him a bride. The photo was necessary because he had left the old country when he was a young man and nobody would recognise him today. He agreed that it might be worth trying, because a lot of his countrymen had found themselves wives this way. But he felt that if he sent a photo of himself, no girl would want to come out to the middle of the bush to marry a man that looked like him. That night, while his friend was asleep, he stole a photo of him and decided that he would have more chance of luring an innocent maiden away from her home with this good looking photo and then when she arrived, it would be too late, she would be here.

He sent the letter and photo off to Greece and waited impatiently for a reply. Eventually he got a letter from his family, saying how good he looked in the photo and that Africa must be doing something good for him to make him that good looking. They also said that they had arranged for a suitable wife for him and that she was on her way by ship to Durban. When he knew the arrival date of his bride to be, he asked his friend to please collect her from South Africa and to bring her to Maun, where the wedding was to take place the day she arrived. He was anxious to get her wed as soon as possible, before she could change her mind. His friend still hadn't missed his photo and had no idea about what had taken place. Knowing that his friend couldn't leave his shop, the good looking fellow agreed to collect the lady in Durban and to bring her straight back to him.

When the bride to be finally arrived in Maun with the good looking friend, the wedding preparations were all ready and the poor girl was whisked straight to the court room where the ceremony took place, before she really knew what had happened. She was a very beautiful woman, with long dark hair and almond shaped eyes. She had a hour-glass figure and was half the age of her groom. This demure Greek beauty came from a very rural family and hadn't had much of an education. She had looked after the family's goats and did menial chores at home, so when they had a chance to wed their daughter to a rich, handsome business man in Africa, her parents jumped at the chance to marry her off.

At the reception in the hotel, the whole story came out and both the new bride and the good-looking friend heard the truth. The fat man said how sorry he was to trick them, but that he knew that if he sent a real photo of himself, nobody would want to marry him. The young girl sobbed her eyes out and said that she wanted to go back home to Greece and her family. The good-looking friend comforted her and danced with her, telling her that it would all work out and that she mustn't be afraid because her husband, although not good looking, was really a good man. They danced out onto the veranda of the hotel and into the night and nobody saw them again, they disappeared.

The party continued throughout the night and into the morning, with much jollity, drinking, singing and breaking of plates. By the time the now very drunk groom, was ready to take his new bride and virgin, to the prepared honeymoon suite in the hotel, he couldn't find her. So it wasn't until mid-morning, after everyone had searched the village high and low, that everyone figured out what had happened. This Greek girl had fallen in love with the man whose photo she had seen while still in Greece and he, on seeing her, had fallen in love too, so they had escaped together, never to be seen to this day.

## Maruti, Dad and Chombo

In his position, Dad had many duties and although I was a small child, I felt that some of them were not good at all, but it was just the way things were in those times and as a child there isn't anything you can do to change things. As an adult, I have looked back many times and have tried to make sense of it, but it still doesn't make any sense at all. I have forgiven my father, whom I love deeply, but I cannot condone what was done in the name of the colonialism of the past. When cases were tried, punishment was meted out and that could be a jail sentence, lashes with a big cruel whip and even hanging, depending on the crimes committed.


## Maruti

Maruti was the biggest, blackest, almost blue-black man I had ever seen, or have ever seen to this day. His big teeth were yellow, as were the whites of his big round eyes, which were also red-rimmed. His hands and feet were enormous and when he walked, the earth trembled. Whenever I see images of King Kong, I remember Maruti, just because of the sheer power he exuded.

Maruti came home to his little hut one day to find a visitor, a family member of his wife's. It was suppertime and Maruti's wife had prepared the evening meal and was serving the visitor as Maruti walked in the door. In their humble abode there was only one plate, which the wife always served her husband's meal on and she ate hers off the saucepan lid. This evening she served the visitor's meal on the plate and after handing him his plate of mielie pap, she served Maruti his meal on the saucepan lid, planning to eat hers after the men had finished their meal. As always, the men in this society were to be respected and the woman took second place. When she handed Maruti his saucepan lid of food, his eyes glowed and a deep primitive growl seemed to come from the pit of his stomach and erupt from his mouth as a howl, screaming what kind of wife was she to serve her husband on a saucepan lid, after he was out at work all day to put food on the table. He flung the food across the mud floor and stormed out of the hut. She thought he had gone off into the bush, but no, he returned with an axe from the woodpile outside and, lifting it above his head, brought it down in the middle of his wife's head, embedding it in the centre of her skull. She just stood there looking at him, not uttering a sound.

She turned around and stepped out of the mud hut and, with the axe handle sticking out over her back, walked to the hospital. The visitor, by this time, had fled as fast as he could out of the mad Maruti's way, in case he got the same treatment. The doctors were amazed when Maruti's wife walked into the hospital with the axe deeply embedded in her head and just a trickle of blood running down the side of her face. They managed to get the axe out of her skull, but when they did, she died immediately. While the axe was embedded, it stopped the bleeding, but once it was released she bled to death straight away and there was nothing they could do to save her. The hospital contacted the police, who went to Maruti's hut and there they found the murderer huddled in a corner, crying like a baby.

Dad was to try Maruti's case, which, of course, was murder. Maruti confessed that he did it in a fit of jealousy and also that his wife didn't respect him, which was very important in native custom. Dad sentenced Maruti to one hundred lashes and a term in prison. I don't remember how long the prison sentence was but I do remember the lashes, because after he was lashed with a leather whip until his big black back was torn like raw meat, Mum would go into the prison and treat his wounds with disinfectant and creams. I doubt whether Dad knew about Mum treating Maruti's back but, as a nurse, I think these things affected her deeply and, as a very humane person, she felt it was her duty to help a man in pain, regardless of his crime. This big black murderer called my Mum 'mummy', like a little boy and was so grateful for her help. He said that he regretted his crime and that he was sorry, but he had to do what a man had to do and now he accepted his punishment like a man.

I will leave Maruti there a while but will come back to him later on, because he becomes very important in my life and ties in with what I am now going to tell you about Dad and Chombo.

## Dad and Chombo

Dad had been trying to control a spate of medicine murders in the area for some time but they were getting worse and the natives were very afraid. There was a chief called Chombo in Maun and it was rumoured that he was capturing small children, killing them and then turning them into *muti* (medicine) by cooking them and using their fat and ground bones, mixed with certain herbs. With these mixtures he would do black magic and his clients would pay good fees for these treatments, either in money, livestock or favours. These treatments and spells could do anything from get you the job you wanted, the woman you yearned for, or a vendetta for an ill done to you in the past. The problem was that nobody could prove a thing against Chombo because nobody wanted to say anything about this old chief, just in case they got into his bad books and were the target of his nasty spells. So there was a sullen silence over the village.

It was a fact that a lot of children were disappearing while out doing errands for their parents, like gathering fruits, herbs or kindling for the fire, usually in the bush, where it was quiet and nobody could see what went on. A lot of little herd boys were the victims too, whilst out with the family goat or cattle herds, again in isolated places. The mothers of these children would come to the police station, which was in the same building where Dad had his offices. It got to be so bad that at one time there was a steady queue every day, of mothers standing patiently awaiting their turn to fill in a form and tell the policeman on duty that, "my son/daughter didn't come home last night". These sad dusty women, with dead eyes, would say no more than that. It was their duty as mothers to report it but looking at their faces you could see that they knew more than they were willing to tell. They were sad and poor and used to life dealing them raw deals; this was just one more. As a child, I knew what was going on because it was the talk of the white community, although us kids didn't know all the details, because the adults spoke in a way we didn't understand. As an adult I have gone over this story many times with my parents. When we were out playing we would frighten each other by saying, "if you don't do this or that, Chombo will come and get you tonight and make *muti* out of you" and then we would go into gory details of how this would come about.

The white children had to be escorted by their nannies and were told not to go out of the yard unless with an adult. African mothers started going everywhere with their children to do the chores, so that their young weren't in isolated places on their own. There were also quite a few women captured by this mad man and they also ended up in the pot, so it wasn't always a guarantee for the children going out with their mothers. Chombo preferred children for his muti because they were tender and the magic worked best if it was from a child and the fatter, the better. The problem was that most of the black children were skinny little things and it was very rare to see a fat picaninny once they had got past that chubby baby stage.

Dad decided to pay Chombo a visit, mainly to see for himself, what this man was like. After all, although these murders were taking place, it was only rumours that Chombo was the culprit. There were informers that had informed the police and there were many who suspected Chombo because they knew what kind of man he was.

Dad and a couple of police officers went to Chombo's village on the outskirts of Maun. They were escorted into a very dark hut by two very big and very scarred thugs. Once they had adjusted to the gloom of the hut, they saw animal skulls and skins hanging from the beams of the thatch above their heads. Just inside the entrance there was a pile of bones in a three legged pot; they could have been animal bones. Chombo was sitting on a throne, dressed in animal skins and dark glasses. He had a zebra-tail fly-switch in his hand, which he was continuously flicking around him to chase the numerous flies away. The hut stank of old, unwashed sweat and kaffir beer, a home-made brew made from fermented maize, both these odours coming from the old chief himself.

Dad was polite to the old man and told him that he was paying him a visit to ask whether Chombo could shed any light on the recent murders. He told Chombo that as he was the chief, he may know what was going on, rather better that the British authorities did. Chombo smiled a greasy smile and was very polite, offering Dad and the policemen a gourd of kaffir beer, which they refused. He told Dad that he was very pleased to have met him and that he would inform Dad of any information that came his way. There was obviously no more to be said at that stage and the thugs, Chombo's right-hand men, ushered Dad and the police out of the hut as quickly as they could.

Once out of the stuffy, smelly hut, Dad took a big gulp of hot dusty air and, blinking in the blinding white light, he took in the clearing of thatched mud huts, situated in the familiar circle, a swept dust clearing with a big cooking pot on the boil, being stirred by a bent woman with a baby tied to her back. The stink of the pot's contents – a greasy, meaty odour – wafted on the afternoon's gritty breeze but then these people ate some strange things. There were several peacocks strutting about and around the huts, opening their beautiful fan tails, showing off their beauty. Dad said that it was almost surreal to see these magnificent birds in this place of suspected evil with a silent foulness in the air.

Dad just had to carry on working with the police, trying to catch the evil man, whether it be Chombo or another, and in the meantime, the killings continued.

After Dad's visit to Chombo, an informer told Dad that Chombo was coming after his daughter... me. According to the informer, Chombo had said that he wanted to teach that white boss a lesson and that he would get his daughter, who was nice and fat and, being white muti, he would get a good price for it. Dad started getting worried that Aggie wasn't going to be enough protection for me, although I reckon that Aggie could frighten anyone off. This is where Maruti comes into the story again.

Chombo's henchmen had been seen hanging around our house. One day when Aggie took me to the other side of the village to play with a friend of mine, these two men followed us. We had walked through the middle of the village, staying where there were a lot of people and Aggie held my hand so tight that it was blue by the time she let go, when we had arrived at my friend's house. When we got home that night, Aggie told Dad what had happened and he made a decision that night to get Maruti out of jail.

Maruti was still in jail at the time of the medicine murders but he was a perfect prisoner and behaving himself like a real gentleman. Consequently Dad got him out of jail during the day to be my bodyguard although at night he had to go back to jail to sleep. One would think it absurd to take an axe murderer out of jail to look after your five-year-old daughter, especially after you had had him whipped to smithereens and locked him up behind bars. You would think that this man would want to get revenge on my father, through harming his daughter or taking the opportunity to escape. I don't know why he didn't do these things. Maybe he was grateful to my mother for the compassion she showed him after his whipping, or maybe, deep down, Maruti was basically a good man, driven in a fit of jealous rage to kill his wife.

A police officer would escort Maruti to our house every morning and collect him every evening, but while he was with me during the day, he didn't have a police escort. I remember the first day he arrived at our house, early in the morning. He knocked timidly on the back kitchen door and Aggie told him to wait until she called Dad. My father told him that he was to look after me and keep an eye out for Chombo's men, whom he knew, as did everyone in Maun by then. He also had to chop the wood and keep the boiler alight and stoked, so that we always had hot water. Taking over some of the chores that the gardener did, meant that the garden boy could help Aggie with the heavy spring cleaning.

I was fascinated by this enormous black man with yellow teeth and red eyes. I would slip out of the house early in the morning while the dewy mists mingled with the smoke from the native's fires. It was the best time of day for me, when the day was new and fresh, with a hint of promise hanging in the air. The early morning smells of mimosa, of mango and mopane, washed sparkling by the dew and so many other aromas tickling the nostrils. The sounds of the river drifting across our sleeping garden, the hippos grunting, the fish eagle splashing into the clear water for its breakfast, the cooing and twittering of hundreds of different birds, the distant greetings of sleepy natives and so much more, music to lull the ears. The night tracks etched into the sand, of insects, of snakes and many other creatures who come out when humans are dead to the world. The magic of an African dawn has no comparison and I loved every one of them.

I would sneak out in my nightie, barefoot and go down to the wood-pile where all the wood was chopped and I would sit there feeling the first rays of the sun on my arms, waiting for Maruti. He would lumber into the yard, closing the squeaky back gate behind him and bidding farewell to his police escort. He would come over to the woodpile and sit on a log next to me. Aggie would bring us a tin mug of tea and a thick doorstep of bread and jam each and we would have our breakfast together in silence, munching, slurping and burping together, adding to all the other animal sounds around us, the steam from our mugs curling up into the blue-grey morning. Maruti would then wipe his mouth with the back of his huge hand, smile at me and ask what we were going to do today. I would tell him that I wanted to go to a friend's house and he would then tell me to go and get dressed while he cut the wood and lit the boiler, ready for the "master's" bath. When he had finished with the boiler, Mum told him where to take me and what time I had to be back for lunch.

I loved walking all over the village, sitting on Maruti's shoulders. I felt as though I was on a big black cloud. My fingers clasped his big prickly head, so that I wouldn't fall off and I could feel the tight springy curls under my little sweaty fingers. My plump, bare brown legs, hanging down over his shoulders, were held in a tight, yet gentle grasp. I could feel his heart beating under my left thigh and his hot breath on my shins as he plodded down the dust road to my friend's house. Maruti walked barefoot and I can remember looking down at his big cracked feet, with the hard yellow nails, that reminded me of rhino horn. With every step, each foot came down with the thud of distant thunder and disappeared into the dust, coming up again, grey and powdery and disappearing again, thud. I watched his feet with a hypnotic fascination, whenever we went on these outings to the village or to my friends' houses.

There were many times when we would see Chombo's men following us at a distance. I think that they must have thought that Maruti was a force to be reckoned with and they were always waiting for the big man to slip up so that they could strike and grab me. But Maruti never let me out of his sight. If I went to a friend's house to play, he would stay in the yard there until I was ready to go home and then he would hike me onto his shoulders again and we would make the trek back home, where he would deposit me safely into our garden and the gates would be locked after us. If we went to the shops, he would carry me all the way and never let go of me. If friends came to my house to play, Maruti would be in the garden watching over us the whole time, without moving. If I was in the house, then he would do chores around the garden.

Maruti had his breakfast and lunch at our place and Aggie would take him a big tin plate of mielie-pap and stew. He would eat it sitting on a big log in the woodpile, under the shade of the pepper-corn trees. Dad would come home for lunch, which was our main meal of the day, so we were supposed to sit together like the perfect family and eat the food that Aggie had prepared for us. It was usually a roast of some sort and vegetables, followed by 364 pudding. I was bored by the adult conversation between Mum and Dad, so I would ask permission to take my food out the back. If Mum was in a good mood, or if she wanted to get rid of me because I was whining, she would say: "Oh go on then... but eat everything on your plate." I would say that I was very hungry and asked for more, which always placated her.

I would carry my full plate out to the woodpile and sit on a log next to Maruti. I would then give him half of my "white people's food" and he would give me a big dollop of mielie-pap and gravy and I would be as happy as a pig in mud. After we had eaten, Aggie would bring us each a mug of tea and Maruti would smoke a rolled up cigarette. Sometimes Dad would give him a pack of "gold leaf", which he loved, but when he had run out, he would roll his own. There were times that I had seen him roll a ciggie with newspaper and leaves from the bush, but that always made him cough and his eyes would water something terrible.

After those lunch breaks, we would sit in the shade while he told me stories. His stories were always of the animals of the bush. These animals could talk and all had their problems and the tales were about how they found solutions to them. I loved those afternoons. Sometimes he would carve little animals out of bits of wood left lying around the woodpile and give them to me after telling me stories about them.

Maruti was an axe murderer and yet there was I, sitting in the middle of a woodpile, with him and an axe. At that time, Maruti was the best friend I had and I loved him. He was so gentle and kind, with the most beautiful smile that I have ever seen on any man. I do not remember how long he was with me but it was until Dad had successfully put Chombo in jail. Eventually Dad had enough evidence to arrest Chombo and the case went to court. This was a big story and judges and lawyers came from Johannesburg, where the case had made the newspapers.

I knew something was going on but the adults were trying to spare us children the gory details. We overheard the grownups when they talked among themselves but they always went quiet if we entered a room while they were talking about the case. It was only when I was older that I heard all the gory details.

The trial was horrendous. Mothers of the murdered children had to hear of the terrible things that had happened. Jars of fat, organs, bones, teeth and skin belonging to the victims were exhibits. Chombo was convicted and sentenced to life imprisonment in South Africa, so the B.P. was to get rid of him altogether, which made everyone breathe a sigh of relief. His henchmen went with him too.

But now I would be without my friend Maruti because I didn't need a bodyguard anymore. He came to say good-bye and cried like a baby and so did I. Dad's gamble had paid off. Maruti had kept me safe. I really missed him when he went back to jail; I was at a loss without him.

When we left Maun a couple of years later, after he was released from jail, he came to say goodbye to us for good and that day, not only Maruti and I cried but Mum and Dad too. I have never forgotten Maruti to this day.


*Schools*

I am going to describe all the schools I went to together, to get it over with, mainly because I wasn't very happy at school, as I felt it interfered with my life as a bush baby and influenced the way I am today.

While I was under the age of six, living in the bush wasn't a problem as far as my education was concerned but when I reached that age the problem had to be faced. The only option was boarding school. I was lucky to go to Maun School at the age of five but at six I had to leave my home in the bush and lose the freedom to roam and it changed me for life.

Altogether I went to six schools, if you count the baobab tree, which I do, because I loved it best and it taught me a lot. I think anywhere that you learn something of value is a school. The baobab tree school was my first school, apart from a crèche I had gone to London before coming out to Africa, but that doesn't count because it wasn't Africa and I was too small to remember it.

## Maun School

Maun School was right opposite our house, which was fortunate for me. I just had to walk across the dust road and I was there. It was a low prefabricated building with a wire fence all around to keep us kids inside. We had large grounds to play in, with swings, a seesaw, a slide and lots of trees to climb. We even had a maypole, which, thinking back now, was a funny thing to have in the bush. I remember the maypole very well because I pushed a little boy around so hard that he fell off and broke his arm, which didn't make me very popular. We had a vegetable and flower garden at the back of the school house too, which we had to plant and care for and the products we took home. I remember that I had to grow sweet-peas and carrots, which bloomed beautifully. This little school was very "Little House On The Prairie" in that all ages were in one class, with only one teacher to teach us. One of the older girls helped the teacher with the little ones and it seemed to work well enough. I remember at that age the work was very basic, the three R's and then we had things like hygiene, nature, singing and music, with little drums and triangles and we even did plays, which the parents came to. I was in a play called "Belling the Cat", an old favourite. My part was a mouse, one of those that had to get the bell on the cat while she slept. A Dutch lady made my mouse costume, which was a fabulous grey, with little pink ears and a long, thick, pink tail, which I could hold and swing like a cabaret star and which I could whip the backs of boys legs with and make them cry. After the play was over, I would walk around Maun in my mouse outfit, sweating in the heat, much to the hilarity of the Africans, but I loved that costume.

Our teacher, whose name I do not remember, was a lovely fat placid woman, with gentle patience. She was also a Quaker, much to the chagrin of a lot of parents, simply because she didn't drink like them, so they thought she was weird, but we kids loved her. She would have tea parties in her house for all her pupils, who weren't many and it was lovely, with a big swimming pool and fantastic garden to play in. She also baked unusual cakes, which my mother never did.

Sometimes she would take us all down to the river on nature walks, where we were to collect all manner of things like porcupine quills, dead insects, snakeskins, seeds, pods, leaves, etc. On these excursions we were to take a picnic with us and we would sit on the river bank paddling our feet in the water, watching the crocs drift by while munching on peanut butter sarnies. We would then all go on to her house, where she would give us a big tea with all her fancy cakes and we could swim until our parents picked us up at the end of the day.

She wouldn't let us swim in the river while we were out with her, because it was too much responsibility. I couldn't understand this at the time, because I was so used to swimming in the river by myself without any grownups around. When I look back now, I realise that even taking us to a place like the croc-infested river in the bush was a risk; I can't imagine any teacher doing that today. What freedom we had.

One day our teacher collapsed in class and a friend and I ran across the road to tell Mum what had happened. They came and took her away, then sent her to South Africa until she got better. I don't know what was wrong with her because the grownups wouldn't tell us, they would just whisper about it. We didn't have school for ages until she came back.

Then I turned six and everything changed. Mum called me in from playing one day and told me that I would be going to big school in Francistown and that I was going to sleep there and have a smart uniform and shiny brown lace-up shoes. She also told me that our neighbour, Janet, a big blonde Scot, was the house-mother there, so she would look after me. Janet had left her husband, so she had got this job at Francistown School. It didn't make a blind bit of difference to me that Janet would look after me, because although we had lived next door to her for two years, I could never understand what she said, her accent was so strong.

We went to see the school and the boarding facilities, which were separate from the classrooms. I wasn't impressed at all.

## Francistown School

So I was packed off to boarding school at the tender age of six. I cried my eyes out when I left Aggie behind and she cried too. It was a long journey through the bush and I was sullen all the way. I couldn't tell the time, nor tie my shoe laces, nor knot the tie I had to wear with my uniform.

I cried every night in my hard little bed and I didn't make any friends. I just sort of drifted through the days, longing for the holidays so that I could go back to Maun and the river. I don't remember much about my stay at that school, probably because I have sort of pushed it out of my memory. Janet was kind but firm to all the kids in her care and didn't treat me in any special way, which was fine by me.

There was man working in the boarding school with Janet, to take care of the little boys who were boarding there. His name was Jan and I was totally in love with him. He was a young fellow with a blond crew cut and a quiff in front of his head, rather like Tin- Tin. He had blue eyes and a lovely smile. He always wore a short safari suit, long socks, with a steel comb sticking out of one of his socks, for combing his quiff and he always wore *veld skoen,* which were always dusty. Jan spoke with a thick Afrikaans accent, which I understood far better than Janet in her broad Scots. All we little girls were in love with Jan because he was always ready to play games and tell us stories, whereas Janet was always too busy and was far too practical to get down on her hands and knees and get dirty with us.

The headmaster was a very obese man in his fifties. He wore ill-fitting suits, even in the heat. He also used to eat bowls of strawberries and cream in class while he was teaching. He had greasy hair that lankly fell over the dirty collar of his shirt, dripping hair oil down the back of his suit jacket. He was creepy. He loved to cane kids for anything. I remember once he was going to cane a boy in a classroom, with the door open so that everyone could see the humiliation of the lad. The boy was bent over a desk with his pants down and the headmaster raised his arm up, ready to bring the cane down on the boy's buttocks, when the boy charged out of the classroom, hiking up his pants as he went. He ran across the courtyard and into another classroom at the other side of the courtyard and locked the door and windows, so his tormentor couldn't get in. The headmaster tried running after the boy, cane in hand, but was so fat that he could hardly walk, never mind run and he was sweating buckets by the time he got to the other classroom. That poor boy stayed in that classroom until the next day, when they called the police to get him out because he was so petrified of the headmaster.

In this man's class was a young girl of ten, a beautiful blonde, blue-eyed, Afrikaans girl. The headmaster asked her parents if he could marry her and they said yes and that it would be a great honour for them if she married him. Although the girl was still a child, she loved the idea that she would be the headmaster's wife and could lord it over all of us. They married, in a big Afrikaans wedding and then he ensconced her in his house within the school grounds and we never saw her again. She became pregnant a month after her wedding at the age of eleven. This poor girl wasn't even allowed to finish her schooling, nor to play with her friends. This was a source of fascination to us and I often wonder what happened to her in the end.

When Dad's overseas leave came around again, we were sent to the village of Machaneng and I was to go to boarding school in Mafeking (today called Mafekeng).

## Convent in Mafeking

Mafeking was famous for its siege and Baden Powell with his scout movement, but none of that mattered to me as a child. I just remember a very daunting looking building surrounded by a tall spiky fence to keep children inside. I was left there by my parents, dressed in my school uniform, together with a big old-fashioned trunk with the school regulation clothes inside and nothing more. There were no comforts packed, as they were not allowed.

This convent was a catholic convent run by the Sisters of Mercy, all Irish. They accepted all denominations, although one could attend Catholic mass if one wanted to. On Sundays we were all divided into our different religions, dressed in our Sunday church dresses, white in summer and navy in winter and we were escorted by the older girls to our respective churches. I loved church, it didn't matter which religion, I loved them all. When Mum and Dad came to the parents evening at the end of term, a Methodist elder said to Mum, "I didn't know Sue was a Methodist," to which Mum replied, "she isn't". My parents soon found out that I had been going to all the churches without the nuns being aware of it. I really enjoyed the church picnics and outings, which involved a lot of eating, especially home-made cakes, because I was always hungry at boarding school, as the food was horrible. The Methodists put on the best show because they would take us to a river for the day where we could swim and bask the sunshine and there were lots of games and a BBQ, with a big tea before they bussed us back to behind bars again, satiated with exercise, food, sun and total freedom.

The nuns were strict and all our time was organised by bells, to get up, to wash, breakfast, exercise class, different lessons, break, meals, bath time, homework, prayers, hair-wash, letter writing time, etc. We were like robots. A lot of us wet our beds, me included, because we were disorientated and missed our families. Our letters were censored so our families never knew how we were and thought it was a good school. I guess it was, up to a point, but there were a lot of very young boarders there, even as young as four.

We were encouraged to do a lot of sport, which I hated. I also took piano lessons, which my mother encouraged because she played, but which I loathed because it took precious playing time away from me. I was never very good at school subjects and never felt that I should be at school at all although I loved art, poetry and the stories of the saints, which were drilled into us. I was a real dreamer. I thought I would make a good nun, so I walked around with a holier than thou look on my face during the holidays, which drove Mum mad.

The convent put on a musical every two years and as I had a good singing voice I was always given one of the main roles. The plays were usually things like 'Snow White and the Seven Dwarfs', 'Sleeping Beauty', or 'Cinderella'. We had professional theatre people out from Johannesburg to direct us and it was a big event. The only problem was that every time we had the play, Dad would get his long overseas leave, so although I went through the rehearsing for months on end, I always had to pull out before the big day of the performance, which made me angry and resentful.

Dad was considered quite a V.I.P. by the nuns, so he would be asked to come all the way from the B.P. to hand out prizes on prize- giving day and to make speeches. I would go home for the holidays, back to the B.P. and then, when it was time to return to the convent, Mum and Dad would try to find someone who was going that way to take me back. Twice I had to go back a couple of days early because that was the only lift available and would save my parents from going all the way to Mafeking. I resented this because not only did I lose two days of my holiday but also I became the only little girl in the huge empty convent and it was creepy. I would sit alone in the big dining room, have a sandwich supper and then go along the long dark corridors to my dormitory, where I would lie in my hard bed and listen to the walls whispering and creaking, with a scratchy blanket covering my head, wishing I were at home.

The convent had been there in the Boer War and there were secret corridors leading to the hospital next door. The wounded troops would be taken from the convent to the hospital through these tunnels. We still had the coir mattresses with bloodstains on them, that we slept on. This old place had quite a history about it and it was definitely haunted. I was often punished by the nuns for one thing or another and my punishment would be to write a thousand lines of, 'I must not (whatever it was I did)', a damned good caning and to stand in the long, dark corridor with my face pushed against the wall, not to move a muscle, the whole night. On these long nights, alone in the corridor, I saw various ghosts and felt them too as they brushed past me. I actually felt that they were there to keep me company and I can't remember being afraid of them. I was more afraid of the nuns, to tell you the truth.

We used to spy on the nuns at night and saw things that, if we told our parents, they wouldn't believe us. We often saw bald headed nuns swimming naked in the swimming pool, cavorting around like whales, whooping it up at midnight, thinking that nobody was watching. We also saw them having a feast one night, tucking into our tuck-boxes. Every term we brought tuck, which was given to us every day after lunch. Kids brought sweeties and chocolates, home-made biscuits, biltong and whatever they wanted from home and the rations had to last us the whole term. We could also buy things from the convent shop if we had pocket money. These holy sisters also liked a tipple, judging by what we saw and by the smell of their breath on occasions.

There was one nun whom I could not stand the sight of because she would always treat me with contempt. She was very dark and slim, with abundant energy. We had spied on her and caught her snogging the priest. They were having a torrid love affair, which we thought was wicked but at the same time titillating.

I had a lovey music teacher, who had become a nun because her fiancé had died in the war, so she had taken the vows and I thought this was so sad and romantic. She was the only nun who could drive. The convent had a big station wagon and this nun used to put on a pair of black leather driving gloves, get into the car and off she would go, speeding down the main street, leaving a trail of dust in her wake. She always came back with a speeding ticket and in the town they called her 'the cowboy nun' but she was a darling and everyone loved her.

I had two special friends in the convent who both came from Ghanzi in the B.P. but other than that, although I got on with everyone, I didn't find it easy to make close friends because I was so used to being by myself in the bush. I was a loner. One of these friends was half Bushman and half Afrikaans, so the other kids used to tease her. She would bring things in her tuck box that the other children didn't understand, but I did. Instead of sweets she would bring things like, roots and desert nuts, dried mopane worms and flying ants. She wasn't interested in our food at all. I liked her because she was a quiet girl and had the bush in her eyes.

The convent influenced me in so many ways, not all of them good. All that discipline, after all the freedom I had enjoyed before, was detrimental. I am in my fifties now and still trying to come to terms with not only the convent but my boarding school experiences in general. I think that boarding school was a colonial institution, part of the deal. My parents knew that if they went out to these territories they would have to send their children to boarding schools, it was just 'the done thing'. I just wish someone had asked me what I thought about it.

Whenever I came back to the convent after a three-month overseas leave, I would be behind with my work and fail miserably, so then I would lose interest because I was always being told off and given extra classes while my friends were out playing. While I was away, my friends would find other friends, as children do, so I would be on my own and have to start from scratch again. If I was asked about my trip, I would tell them but because we went back on the Union Castle ships and had the opportunity to stop on the way in lots of exotic places, I would tell them of all the places I had visited and things I had seen, which made me sound like a show-off. I couldn't win.

The Convent was the last school I attended while my parents lived in the B.P. when we lived in Machaneng and Molepolole, so I would go back to these little villages for my holidays.

When independence came to the B.P., on 30<sup>th</sup> September 1966, we went back to England, where I was a stranger and a foreigner. Dad put me into a very expensive and posh girls' school in Newcastle-upon-Tyne (he was working at the university there), thinking it would make up for all the upheaval he had caused in my life with his moving. Unfortunately, he was wrong. The girls there were so posh, polished and well-dressed, whereas I had come from the bush, badly dressed and badly informed as to the workings of a modern society in the sixties. Everyone was talking about the Beatles and the Rolling Stones but the only beetles I knew of were insects that rolled big balls of dung over real rolling stones. I was the laughing stock once again, but that is another story.

After being in the UK for two years, Dad had a yearning to go back to Africa, so he got a job in Sierra Leone, which meant another boarding school for me in South Africa and it was a strict Afrikaans school, run by staunch supporters of the apartheid regime. I will tell you about that experience later on. My brother was lucky in that he never had to go to boarding school because by the time he went to school my parents were living in civilization where there were local day schools.

I hated every minute of my schooldays and I think that what I learned in the bush was the best schooling for me, simply because I was happy. There is so much to learn from nature and although it probably doesn't do you much good if you live in the city. I think there are very real values to be learnt from living with nature. Although I have felt hard done by in many ways, by my parents' choices involving me, I have to feel grateful for the experiences I had in the bush, which I saw it at its best, before it was destroyed by progress. I have probably been to the best school in the world.

Dad in the official "ice-cream" suit.

Dad ,Tom, Jackson and Hallet.

Our house in Kasane.

Our Machaneng house and garden.

Our house and garden in Molepolole.

Meeting with the bushman.

Mum, Dad and Little Tom at a stop over break in the Kalahari Desert.

River bank Kasane me and Jaggers.

Sleeping under the stars in the desert.

Swimming pool in the bush.

Tom, lending a helping hand.

Tom in Maun garden, enjoying the sun.

Shasha, Russian diva of the bushveldt.

Mum and I on *Pretoria Castle* on our first trip out from England to Africa.

# 6.   Machaneng

Machaneng was our next station and, to tell you the truth, it doesn't stay in my memory as anything special. I guess that by this time I was getting older and was away at boarding school most of the time. I do remember it being a remote place of dust and thorn trees, nothing like the bustling life we had in Maun. Our house was the standard government house and the garden was big. I say 'garden' but it was more like a front yard and back yard because not very much grew there. We had a lot of cacti and scrubby little bushes, which were broken up with the colour of Syringa, jacaranda, poinsettia and bougainvillea, all of which seemed to thrive without any care and even less water. Our house backed onto an old airstrip that was overgrown with weeds and occasionally the prisoners would come and clear it if a plane wanted to land, usually a little aircraft and sometimes an old Dakota would make an appearance. Dad and I would walk along the airstrip with a notebook and binoculars to bird spot, because there were a lot of very interesting birds there.

Our house was surrounded by a wire fence and if you stood at the bottom of the yard, you looked over the African village below in a valley. There were all these little thatched mud huts that always seemed to be swathed in a grey mist that was really just the cooking fires kept lit permanently outside their huts,.

Just out of our front gate were Dad's office and the police station, which was handy because Dad just stepped out of our house and into his office. There was also a mud hut with a thatched roof similar to those the natives lived in, which was empty. The door to this hut was kept padlocked, which intrigued me no end.

## Mohampi

Aggie was there for us as always and we had a new addition to our family, Mohampi or 'Jackson', as he liked to be called. Jackson was very black, with a permanent wide smile and dancing eyes. He also had a huge nose with enormous nostrils, which he always seemed to have a finger in. He was a slow, bumbling character who took life as easy as he could, which used to annoy Mum and Dad terribly. He loved playing with my little brother and would take him for piggybacks down the long dirt track to the Indian-run shop that sold everything. Mum would give him a shopping list to hand to the Indian shopkeeper because he couldn't read but would forget everything if she just told him what to buy. This little store was one of those that sold everything and always had a crowd of Africans milling around outside the entrance. Mum had an account there and at the end of the month would pay it off, because it was easier to send the servants to do the shopping that way, with no money changing hands. One day Jackson and my little brother had gone to the store on an errand for Mum and besides all she asked him to buy, Jackson had bought two plastic babies' feeding bottles, one in acid green and the other in fluorescent pink. When Mum asked him why he had added that to the list, he told her that a baby like Tom should have pretty coloured bottles instead of those dull glass ones. Tom loved them of course and Mum couldn't take them away from him. Jackson's heart was in the right place.

Jackson did a bit of everything and helped out everywhere, always with a smile. He would do a bit in the garden and then help in the kitchen, or the laundry, or fix things that needed mending, although he did the ironing better than he did the mending of things. Mum had to entertain visiting VIPs sometimes and then Jackson would be all decked out in a starched white uniform and told to serve the canapés at cocktail parties or serve at table whenever we had a dinner party. Mum would give him lessons in how to serve and what cutlery went where but all this did for Jackson would be to set him off into a fit of giggles. Mum fired Jackson every day and he would just say, "yes Madame" and then come to work the next morning as if nothing had happened. Mum didn't have the heart to really sack him.

When we went to our next station, Molepolole, two years later, Jackson joined Aggie in following us there because he had become part of our family by that time and little Tommy loved him. Jackson's best job of all was babysitting and playing with my baby brother because he was just a big baby himself.

In Machaneng we also had two of Aggie's sons with us, Nani and Juliman, who were about eight and ten. At the back of our yard we had a few huts that Aggie and her family lived in and a hut for Jackson too, so firing him wasn't really an option.

### Violet's Bicycle

Machaneng was a boring place compared to Kasane and Maun because the rivers in those previous places were a continuous source of entertainment, whereas this place was in the middle of nowhere, with nothing to do. I suppose it was a good thing that for most of the year I was away at boarding school, although I didn't think so at the time. When I was at home for the holidays, I used to walk into the African village and I made a friend of a nurse from the local African clinic, called Violet, a lovely coloured lady with gentle manners and a soft voice. She lived in one of the typical mud huts and when I went to visit her she gave me mugs of hot tea with condensed milk in and pieces of thick, ash-baked sponge cake, which we would dip into our sickly sweet tea, while she told me stories about her life.

Parked outside her hut was her bicycle, a very big, old fashioned, black bike, which she would ride to work on, visiting all the sick people in their huts. On the front of the bicycle she had a basket in which she would put her black medical bag, with all the equipment she needed for work. I was intrigued by this bicycle because I had never had one and didn't know how to ride it, so one day she offered to teach me. She lowered the seat, but even then, my little legs could only just make the pedals. I would go to her hut every day for bicycle lessons and then one fine day I could do it on my own and I rode Violet's bike all around the village, through the dust, leaving tyre marks and scattered chickens in my wake. Of course, after that, I nagged my parents' silly until they bought me a bike the following Christmas, but, although I have had a few bikes since then, there has never been a bicycle to match Violet's big old black bike.

*Neighbours*

Next door, to our left, lived an agricultural inspector with his wife and three children, two boys and a girl. We became good friends and that relieved the boredom during the holidays. We put a big petrol drum on each side of the wire fence separating our gardens, so that we could just climb over to play, instead of going out the front gate and doing a detour around the bush to each other's houses.

There was a big farm not too far from us that belonged to a white Afrikaner family. They were cattle ranchers and very wealthy. I loved going to visit this family because they had a swimming pool and a tennis court and their huge garden was always green and lush, with lots of trees and flowers. They had an irrigation system and a reservoir, not like our measly water tank at the back of the house. They had a lot of low ranch- like buildings on their property which were the main living quarters of the house and their grown-up children, who lived in South Africa, had their own houses too on the property. There was the games room, which was more of a house than a room. And there were dozens of bathrooms scattered around the property, all beautifully decorated, as was the rest of the house. These people gave fantastic parties, where all their farmer friends would be invited and we had the run of the farm because they loved kids and, having lost a son to lightning, they loved having children around the farm. They would entertain on a large scale and everything was brought in from neighbouring South Africa, everything except the meat, which was their own and cooked on a big spit in the garden by the men. They even brought bands in from South Africa when they put on a dance, usually at Christmas and New Year. At this time of year, we would often sleep over in one of the luxury guest houses so that the grownups could drink solidly without stopping and not have to drive home drunk and ending up in a *donga*,[1] which happened quite a lot out there.

The Christmas presents that these people bought for their guests and the children were not your usual bottle of plonk or box of old chocolates. They would buy jewellery, good whiskey, real silver and gold items like cigarette lighters and pens, etc, and the kids would get beautiful dolls and bikes. So, as you can imagine, we loved going to the farm to visit Uncle Dick and Aunty Emmy, as they were called. I always wished that I could live like them.

There was something that we had, however, and they didn't, a flagpole, which made up for everything our place lacked. I always felt that we were the bee's knees having the flagpole in our garden. Every morning at sunrise, a policeman dressed in Khaki, with a big felt hat and leather strap under his chin, would march into our garden with the union jack rolled up under his arm. He would stand to attention and salute and then he would hoist the flag up the flagpole, where it would hang limply in the heat, as if exhausted by its mere hoisting. He would salute again and then march off, very proud in his bearing and the fact that he had the important job of hoisting the flag at the D.C's residence. In the evening he would do the same in reverse, taking the flag down. We were the only house with a flag and I felt a certain degree of self-important snobbishness about it. I don't feel the same way about it today. I remember it fondly but what it represented in colonial Africa is

---

[1] A dried-up watercourse or small ravine.

not what moves me. My feelings at the time were those of a child showing off, nothing more.

*Entertaining*

As I have said before, Mum and Dad had to entertain whenever visiting dignitaries had business to do in the area. We had our fair share of prime ministers from other African states, bishops and other religious figures from different religions, representatives from many countries around the world, writers and film-makers and even royalty. Poor Mum, on a very meagre government budget, had to do the best she could and just hope that these visitors would look around them and realise that living in a place like this we couldn't do more than we did. Whenever Mum heard of a pending visit she would go to the back door at the kitchen and shout out into the yard, "Jackson, Aggie, shoot another potato!" which meant, 'get ready for visitors'. There were never any complaints following the visits, so I guess it meant that all went well.

I remember once, we were expecting a member of the Royal family, I think it was Princess Alice, but being a child at the time, I thought it was the Queen of England. We were taught how to curtsy and the men how to bow and all Mum's dresses had to be so many inches below the knee. There was a long list of protocol do's and don'ts, which got everyone in a fair tizzy for weeks in advance of the visit. I don't remember the visit itself because they tucked me away out of harm's way, just in case I did something untoward or caused something to go wrong.

I do remember Sir Seretse Khama[2] coming to stay overnight whenever he and his wife Ruth were in the area. He and Dad

---

[2] Sir Seretse Khama, KBE (1 July 1921 – 13 July 1980) was a statesman from Botswana. Born into one of the more powerful of the royal families of what was then the British Protectorate of Bechuanaland, and educated abroad in neighbouring South Africa and in the United Kingdom, he returned home – with a popular but controversial English bride – to lead his country's independence movement. He founded the Botswana Democratic Party in 1962 and became Prime Minister in 1965. In 1966, when Botswana gained

were good friends and had an Oxford education in common. I used to play with their children sometimes when we went to visit them in Serowe, but that wasn't as often as Seretse and Ruth coming our way, without the children, on official business. Whenever they stayed at our place it was an excuse for a party, although poor Seretse was a diabetic, which made things very difficult for him.

I remember that in our house we had one of those old fashioned (by today's standards) black telephones that you had to dial by putting your fingers in the little holes and drag the dial around. We were on a party line, as everyone in the area was, which meant that everyone had their own ring signal and although the phone would be ringing all day, you only picked up the receiver when you heard your signal, or else you would be in the middle of someone else's conversation. Us kids used to listen into some really juicy conversations between illicit lovers and crooked business dealings, until we were caught at it and punished. On one occasion when Ruth and Seretse were staying, Mum put them in the guest room, where the only telephone in the house was situated, on the bedside table, which also acted as a potty cupboard, with a potty inside. After a heavy night of drinking, when everyone had staggered off to bed, I heard the phone ringing during the night from my bedroom next door, followed by a lot of bashing about and swearing and then silence. The next morning at breakfast, a very sheepish Seretse told Mum that he had found the telephone in the potty. I don't know whether the potty was used or not, but it had obviously been keeping him awake during the night and he had slammed the phone into the cupboard with the potty in it. Everybody had a good laugh about it.

Mum and Dad were invited to Seretse's investiture, which I am told was very moving, although I was at boarding school at the time. Both Sir Seretse Khama and his delightful English wife

independence, Khama became its first president. During his presidency, the country underwent rapid economic and social progress. [*Source:* Wikipedia]

Ruth were lovely people and only did good for their country, which is reflected in the continued progress Botswana has made from Seretse's time right up to the present day. He was not only a noble chief to his people but a gentleman to all, with an educated foresight into the needs of his country. With an English education behind him, he was a great negotiator and was respected by one and all. Unfortunately he passed away too young, but he left a legacy to be proud of.

*My Little Library*

The little round thatched hut that was kept under lock and key was going to gain new life. Mum suggested to Dad that we should start a library for the few white inhabitants of Machaneng so the servants were rallied and told to repair the thatch and clean the hut. This really only meant sweeping the dung floor, cleaning the one window and airing the place out; there wasn't anything in the hut to clean. Shelves were put up around the curved walls and a table and chair were brought from our house. Mum started by taking all our old books in and then we went around all the white people's houses, asking for old books, which they donated. There weren't many to start with but as time went on, more books arrived. We were sent books from grandparents and when we had read them we would take them into our library and everyone did the same. If anyone went to another place, they always bought books back with them and that was always an excitement. Mum put a sign on the door saying the hours the library was open and put everyone's name down in a big book, with the date and titles of the books taken out.

I loved this little library and thought that it was mine. I would sometimes take the key and sneak off to open the library door and then lock myself in. Inside it was dark and cool. The little window didn't give much light and one had to leave the door open to see better when choosing books. There was a musty smell, which was a mixture of old books, old mud walls and dung floor. I would take out a book and sit cross-legged under the little window, leaning my back against the cool mud and would spend hours there, mulling over the old pages. It was cool and silent, apart from the crackling noises in the thatch above, made by all the little animals and insects that made their homes within the straw. I loved that little sanctuary, far away from the noisy, dusty, white heat of the world outside, where I was cocooned in a world of my own. I have loved books and solitude ever since.

## Snakes

Snakes had always been around us from the time we had arrived in Africa but for some reason I remember seeing far more snakes in Machaneng than in any other place we lived. Dad used to either whip them dead, cut their heads off with his ceremonial sword or, if he had a gun handy, shoot them. When I was younger, in Kasane, I would pick up any snake that crossed my path and take it into my bedroom without telling a soul, which, thinking about it now, was a pretty risky thing to do. As I got older, however, I became more aware of their danger, thanks to the grown-ups. My little kitten Chloe was killed by a snake and that really put me off them in a big way. We had to be very careful where we walked in the bush because they were everywhere and I never wore shoes. We also used to climb trees and had tree-houses and swings high up in the big trees, so we had to be very careful and check first before climbing. If you heard the birds going crazy, it was a warning that there was a snake in the area.

The real problem was when the snakes came into the house, which was often. I can remember one day we had seen a snake going into the house but when we tried to go after it, it disappeared and we couldn't find it. Dad was away on a trip so it was just Mum, Tom and I at home. That night Mum lit a paraffin lamp and left it by her bed and also left Dad's big whip next to the bed. She must have dozed off and when she awoke with a start, she saw this thing crawling up the wall, so she screamed blue murder, which made me run into her room where she was standing on the bed, as white as a sheet. There was no snake but the shadow of the whip had looked like one and on awakening she had got the fright of her life, thinking it was the snake we hadn't found earlier in the day. That was the trouble with not having electricity, you couldn't just switch on a light in an emergency. And you always had to shake out your shoes before putting them on, just in case.

I went to the toilet one day and right behind the cistern was a black mamba asleep next to the cool tank. I had got off the very high, old-fashioned toilet seat and was about to stand on the seat to reach the chain to flush, which was the only way I could reach it, when I saw this snake coiled up. I stepped quietly off the seat and decided to leave the flushing and get out as quickly as possible. But I was locked in the loo and couldn't get the door open. I was afraid to scream for help in case I woke the snake up and Mum was asleep, having her afternoon siesta. I sat in the corner sweating for ages, until Mum got up and wanted to go to the loo. I heard her try the door and then I whispered to her, telling her of my predicament. She called for Jackson, who managed to get the door open and also killed the snake by throwing a big rock on its head before it woke up. Jackson thought it was a very funny situation and went around for a week giggling whenever he saw me. Black mambas are deadly, so I didn't see the funny side of it at all.

One evening Mum and Dad were having sundowners in the garden and I was sitting with them, telling them what I had been doing during the day, when Dad suddenly told us to be very quiet. He got up, picked up the whip by his chair and walked towards the house. Mum and I turned around to see where he was going, when we saw an enormous cobra at the entrance of the house. When Dad got close to the snake, he raised the whip above his head, ready to bring it down and decapitate the creature. As Dad brought his arm down, the cobra swung around and raised half its body in the air, with its hood completely open, ready to strike. One has to be careful because a cobra can spit venom from quite a distance and can blind you. Mum and I were completely paralysed with fear as we watched in stunned awe this death dance between the cobra and Dad, each advancing and withdrawing, as the other attacked. Just then, our dog Tuli came bounding around the house and the cobra was distracted for a moment by the noise, giving Dad the chance to bring the whip down and break its vertebrae. This was a proud moment for Dad and another notch in his belt.

Behind our house we had a big metal water tank that collected rainwater, which wasn't often, but there always seemed to be a trickle when one opened the tap. One hot afternoon I was playing in the back yard while Dad was at work and Mum was having a rest. It was one of those sultry days with the distant rumble of thunder that doesn't usually produce anything more than dark clouds and a heavy lethargy upon all living creatures. I went to the water tank for a drink and as I put my head under the tap for a quick slug of water, my eye caught a glimpse of a huge python curled up between the wall of the house and the water tank. I stood up, forgetting about my thirst and just stood staring at this beast with fascination. It was huge and wound into a perfect spiral, with its big flat head resting on its coiled body. It was obviously asleep and had gone to the tank to keep cool. Its skin had the most beautiful markings in browns, black and cream, with a pattern that looked as though it had been painted by hand. I crept slowly away until I was out of the front gate and then I ran as fast as I could to Dad's office and told him what I had seen. He grabbed a shotgun from the police department and we went back to the water tank. I half expected the snake to have gone and then Dad would never believe me and say that I had exaggerated the size but the python was still there, just as I had left him. Dad gave a low whistle at the size of the snake, took aim and fired. The noise was shattering and Mum came running out of the house, worried sick at what she would find on hearing the shot. The sight that met her wasn't exactly pretty. There was Dad, gun in hand, splattered in blood and the wall of the house looked as though there had been a massacre, blood and guts splattered all over it. He had blasted the snake at such close range that it had exploded. I was just glad that it couldn't have been aware of what had hit it, as I felt sorry for it.

There were a lot of harmless snakes around too, but it was difficult on first sighting to distinguish a tree snake from a green mamba, or a mouse snake from a black mamba. We became experts though, through necessity. There were also puff adders around and they were the same colour as the earth, which made them easy to step on. Machaneng was rife with all sorts of snakes and our chickens and pets were always being killed by them, so it was a constant worry while out playing and we also had to check the house continually as they would frequently come in and hide in toilets, cupboards or under the bed.

I heard a story of an African woman who went to bed every night with her baby by her side. The baby was getting weaker and cried a lot and the woman didn't know what was wrong with the child, nor why it was getting thinner when she could feel the baby suckle at her breast while in bed. One night she awoke to feel her breast being suckled, but at the same time the baby was howling out loud. She reasoned that the baby couldn't be howling and yet at the same time be sucking at her breast and when she sat up, she saw that it was a snake that was attached to her breast and it had been the snake that had been taking all the milk every night while her baby had gone hungry. Once the snake had been killed, the baby put on weight and became contented again. There were also a lot of stories of snakes suckling cows and goats at night. Apparently, they love milk.

*Holidays*

As I have mentioned before, we had a three-month overseas holiday every two years, which really messed up my schooling and friendships although I enjoyed the cruises back and forth between South Africa and England, and all the exotic places we stopped at on the way. I also enjoyed the long trip from Bechuanaland Protectorate to Cape Town, where we spent a couple of days before boarding the ship for our trip. Once we got the ship from Beira in Mozambique, which was fun because it was a Portuguese colony and the food and the language were so different and foreign that it didn't feel like we were in Africa at all, which was a treat after coming from the bush. Eating curried prawns on the beautiful sandy beaches, listening to *fado* was like walking into another life altogether.

Apart from these trips to and from England we had very few breaks, as far as I can remember. While we were in the UK, we stayed with my grandparents in the Isle of Wight and while there we would make day trips to all the things worth seeing and doing, then we would do the same in Wales while visiting the other side of the family. Mum always said that the real holiday was on the ship, far away from family altogether. I must admit though, that I loved seeing my cousin in Blaenavon, who was older than me but I really loved her and thought she was so sophisticated, as far away from a bush baby as you could get. She lived a fairly sheltered life in the village and said, years later when we were adults, that she envied me my life, whilst I, on the other hand, always envied her, because she had the stability I craved, which she said, stifled her. The grass is always greener on the other side.

While we were living in Machaneng and I was at boarding school in Mafeking, I do remember two trips we made that were not on the way to get a ship or to go to England. My parents had friends who had rented a house in the Wilderness in South Africa and they asked us if we would like to go too. I don't remember anything much about that holiday except the beaches because they were empty of people, completely virgin and pristine. It is a beautiful part of the world, even today, but at that time there were less houses and buildings around and it was as if the world was new. I do remember that Dad was nearly eaten by a shark there. We were sitting on the beach, the women talking, us kids playing in the sand, when Dad said he was going in for a dip. The husband of Mum's friend had gone somewhere to buy something, so he wasn't around at that moment. Dad has always been a powerful swimmer and comfortable in water. He swam out further and further until we could just see his little head as a black blob in the distance. Suddenly his arms started flailing around in the waves and he started swimming back at quite a pace. Mum and her friend were watching this and were talking about it, Mum beginning to worry. Then we saw a fin following Dad. We watched in terror, not knowing what to do. There was nobody around and there were no such things like lifeguards then, nor mobile phones, we were completely on our own. We watched this scene, feeling absolutely helpless. Dad swam as fast as he could but we couldn't see him making progress. Eventually he made it to shore with all his limbs intact but totally exhausted. He said he didn't think he would make it because the tide was pulling him out. The currents are very strong on that coast; it is very wild and dangerous. Sharks are plentiful off the South African coast. This one followed Dad right up the beach until he could stand and then it veered off and went back to the deep. Why it didn't attack him, I don't know, because it could have. Dad lay on the beach trembling, thanking God he had made it. A couple of my friends were mutilated by sharks off the South African coast, so it is a very real fear.

One Easter holiday when the schools were off for two weeks, Dad said he had a surprise for us; he was taking us to Natal for a holiday. We hired a cottage by the sea within a holiday complex in Shelly Beach, off the Natal coast. I was so excited because I was going to do what the other kids at school did, go on a normal holiday to the seaside. Mum and Dad picked me up from boarding school in our old Land Rover and we drove down to Natal, stopping to sleep on route at these old colonial hotels, rather like the one in Maun. For meals on route we would stop at Portuguese cafes with names like, The Polana Café, The

Lisboa, or Madeira, where we would order mixed grills that included, T-bone steak, boerewors,[3] bacon, egg, fried tomato, baked beans, mushrooms, chips, fried bread and salad, all served on huge oval platters and surrounded by salad. All this I would wash down with a 'brown cow' – an ice-cold Coca-Cola with a big blob of ice cream on top. We would buy lots of sweets, drinks, chocolates, fruit, biltong[4] and crisps for the journey and then wondered why we were sick and had to stop to get rid of it all. Life was fantastic then, before we all started worrying about things like keeping a good figure or cholesterol.

We would play games of "I Spy" or counting different coloured cars and sing "Ag pleeez Daddy" till we got to the sea, which was always magic after the dust of Machaneng. We went out for big South African meals in restaurants, bought gaudy costumes, buckets and spades and hats with "I love Durban" on them and best of all were the drive-in movies. There was a feast of Elvis movies on at the time and there was a drive-in near our cottage, so Dad would take us every night (under sufferance, I must say) until we had seen all the Elvis movies being shown. I think it was one of the best holidays I have ever had. I think my parents also enjoyed it, probably for the mere fact that they got away from Machaneng.

Other than that, I don't remember any other getaways, apart from our shopping trips to Rhodesia, when we lived in Kasane, but they were not really holidays, just shopping trips. But I do think that any break away from the villages where we lived was a relief.

Dad often had to visit farmers in the area, tribal chiefs too. Some of these trips would take him away for a couple of weeks and sometimes we would go with him. Many times we would be invited to stay at the farmers' homes, where they would treat us

---

[3] Boerewors is a sausage, popular in South African cuisine. The name comes from the Afrikaans words *boer* (farmer) and *wors* (sausage).
[4] *Biltong* is a kind of cured meat that originated in South Africa. Many different types of meat are used to produce it, ranging from beef through game meats to fillets of ostrich.

like royalty and I loved it when we did that because I love farms. Whenever we stayed at a farm, the farmers would fill our truck with whatever they grew, sacks of fruit, nuts, vegetables, etc. They were always so hospitable and generous.

Many more times, we would camp out under the stars. I would lie in my camp bed and listen to the roaring of lions, the grunting and snuffling of different animals, while looking up at a star-laden sky, with no light pollution to spoil it. To awaken in the early morning with the dew on your face and sip hot coffee while watching the bush take on a new day is magic. I remember once we went on one of these trips with Dad and a policeman. When the policeman awoke in the morning he had a hole in his stomach and there was an African cricket eating him. It was horrible and made you realise that there is a lot out there to be wary of.

*Oddballs*

It is amazing the strange characters you found living in the bush. I often wonder if the bush made them strange or whether they were strange to start with and that is why they went into the bush.

I have already mentioned our friends Sacha and her husband Sidney and the Greek who ordered a wife from his home country but there were strange people everywhere we went – and a mixture too. There were the posh Brits working for the government who thought that they were there to save the planet and that everyone had to obey them, their servants and children alike. Their social activities were drinking a lot and acting the fool most of the time, at least that is what I thought when I was a little girl. I just couldn't fathom out why responsible adults had to act that way and I felt a tremendous sense of responsibility for my parents and their friends after they had had too much to drink. A lot of them were sleeping around too, swapping partners. This I gleaned from snippets of overheard adult conversations, confirmed later when I was considered old enough to know of such things.

Then there were the young single men, generally British or South African, usually dressed in khaki safari suits and working in posts under the District Commissioner. They were either very tanned from being out in the bush, if they were South Africans, or very red from being out in the bush, if they were British. They all drove Land Rovers or trucks and were all cocky, all randy as hell and all drank heavily. They were also very lonely, living in the outback of nowhere.

If there was a party where a young, single female was present, usually someone's visiting relative on holiday, they would swoop down on the poor girl like a flock of vultures. At the mission stations there would often be young VSOs doing a stint at the missions and they were constantly pestered by these young studs. It didn't matter that some of these girls were as ugly as sin, they were available. One such young VSO[5] from England was quite flattered by all the attention she was getting from all these macho men, because at home I am sure she wouldn't have got much attention at all, not being very pretty. She slept with every one of these men but the sad thing was that they talked about her in intimate detail whenever they gathered for sundowners.

In one village where we lived, we had a young policeman from Scotland living next door to us. This man used to invite my little brother Tom, who was about four years old at the time, to lunch every Friday. His servant would prepare a lunch of bangers and mash (it never varied) for them and they would eat it and afterwards stand on their heads, supporting their legs against a wall and pick their noses together, Tom in his little grubby shorts and Bill in his policeman's uniform. Now if that's not strange, I don't know what is!

---

[5] VSO (Voluntary Service Overseas) is a development charity that sends volunteers to work abroad.

In the same village, lived three Johns, whom I will call John A, John B and John C. John A, was in an agricultural post and lived alone. He was a big fat, blond fellow with a very red face that resembled a pig. The poor guy couldn't help that, I know, but he ate and drank like one too. In the end he committed suicide through total loneliness. Further on down the same street was John B. This man was in his sixties with long grey hair and a terribly posh British accent. He had been in the British navy and ran his little house like a ship, decorated it like a ship, controlled his servants as if they were the crew of his ship and even wore his navy uniform and walked around with a periscope and a compass. We used to ask him the time and he would look up at the sun and tell us, instead of looking at a watch. I don't remember what his job was and he was always at home, never in an office or out in the bush like other men. I do know that I felt strange being around him. When Mum and I went for walks past his house, he would come out for a chat and then ask Mum to leave me at his house for lunch. Luckily, Mum didn't trust him, so she always made an excuse not to leave me there.

John C was a completely different character and everyone loved him. He was an elderly widower with a bad stutter. When he got drunk he would sing, without stuttering at all, and his favourite song was "O Come All Ye Faithful", which I can't hear today without thinking of him. John was a vet and travelled all over the area, checking animals on farms and wild animals in danger. He was also a lonely man and missed his wife terribly but as everyone loved him he was invited to houses for meals and also entertained a lot at his home.

He had a son Mark, of about sixteen, who was at boarding school in South Africa and who would come out for school holidays. I had a big crush on Mark. He was a big lad for his age and very dark, with ruddy cheeks and long eyelashes. Mark was very macho but in a nice way and would help his Dad a lot and anyone who needed it. He kept a python in his underwear drawer and one day the maid opened the drawer to put away his clean clothes and when she saw the snake, she fled, never to come back. Mark and I laughed like drains but John wasn't amused because he had to find another maid.

John also had a bull-terrier called Debbie who was a real softie. Debbie slept in the same bed as John and when the maid brought the morning tea in on a tray, it had to include an extra saucer because Debbie would have her saucer of tea with John before they got up for breakfast. John loved his Debs, as he called her and went everywhere with her in his truck. One day while they were out in the bush, Debbie disappeared and John couldn't find her, so he came back home without her, heartbroken. He would come around to our house every evening and cry his eyes out and was lonelier than ever.

Three months after Debs had disappeared, John had to go out into the Kalahari Desert again, to do a job. As he was driving through the bush a bushman dressed only in animal skins waved him down. This little wrinkled man had his bow and arrows slung over one thin shoulder and he was jumping up and down trying to stop John's truck. John pulled up and asked the man what was wrong, thinking that he needed help. The Bushman gestured to John to follow him, which he did, slowly over the scrubby bush, until they came to a clearing where there were more bushmen sitting around a fire. John got out of the truck to see what these people wanted, when the man who led him there, went into a little hut made of sticks. When he came out again, he had Debbie in his arms. Debs jumped out of the bushman's arms and ran to John, who scooped her up into his arms, crying and kissing her all at once.

Debbie was fat and sleek, so she had been looked after very well by these ancient people. They knew of John and the good person he was, so when they found Debbie in the dessert, shortly after John had lost her, they decided that they would look after her until he came back one day, which they knew he would. Debbie was on the front page of a South African newspaper, with the title of "Debbie, the bush dog returns home". And what a welcome Debs had when John got her home. He gave a big party to celebrate her return.

My brother Tom's godfather, Willy, was also a funny little character. He worked for the Public Works Department and was in charge of maintaining all the government houses in working order. He was from Yorkshire and had come out to Africa after a failed marriage. I remember one day he had to knock on all the doors to let everyone know that the houses were due to be repainted. He had a colour chart with him, which he showed Mum. She was excited at the choice of colours, because after all, life could be pretty dull in the bush, so a bit of colour would be more than welcome. She made Willy a cup of tea while they mulled over the chart and then she said, "Willy, I can't decide between these two colours because, although they are completely different, I like the two of them,"

Willy looked over his cup at her and said in his Yorkshire accent, "you can choose whatever colour you like, but you'll get Stone/Opal." He had been given great vats of this yucky colour and had been told to use it to paint all the houses. He had brought the colour chart out from England with him and merely used it to blag a cup of tea, a drink, or even a meal out of each visit.

On the outskirts of Kasane there was a solitary Welshman living in the middle of the bush, a real hermit. He had worked for the British government when younger but since his wife had died and he retired he preferred to stay out in the bush by himself. He was a lovely gentle man and we would get him things in Rhodesia when we did our shopping. He would never accept an invitation for a meal or a drink but would always like us to stay for a meal with him and he was a fantastic cook. His bread was out of this world.

There was a Greek man who lived in the bush in a native village with the black people. Dad had to go out there sometimes to see the tribal chiefs and Mum and I would go with him. This was before Tom was born. I can remember the first time we went there, we got out of the truck and there in a clearing, sitting in a rocking chair, in the middle of nowhere, sat this good-looking young Greek man. He had dark curly hair, big black eyes and a golden body. He was wearing only a pair of shorts and no shirt. Across his lap lay a shotgun. He didn't bother to get up and greet us, so Dad went up to him and introduced himself and told him that he was in the area to see the chief. The man wasn't interested in what Dad had to do in the area but asked if we would like to stay for supper. Dad said thank you very much, that would be very nice indeed. Dad's impeccable British good manners were lost on this fellow and he didn't even look up. Instead, he aimed his gun at the scrawny chickens that were scratching the dirt and fired, one, two, three, four, in total, all dead in the first shot. He then clicked his fingers and a black woman came and picked up the chickens, which she flung into a big black three-legged pot full of boiling water, to loosen the feathers before plucking them. When they were done she put them all on a long stick and they were roasted over a big fire.

We joined the Greek, sitting around the fire where the chickens were being spit-roasted. Once the man got talking he was quite friendly and told us all about his life. He had become fed up with civilization, had come to live in the bush years ago and had been living there ever since. He had several black women at his disposal and had fathered a lot of children by different women. There were many children running around the huts who were very light skinned with hair like his rather than the typical African head of hair. We went back quite a few times after that and he was always seated in his old rocking chair in the clearing in front of the huts. When he saw us arrive, he would wave us over and pot-shot some chickens. This routine never changed and we never ate anything else but it is the best chicken I have ever tasted.

Someone told us that before we arrived in Maun, there was a Greek barman at the hotel and one night, as he was drying glasses behind the bar, he looked up as a stranger entered the bar. On seeing this man, the Greek bar tender put down the glass he was drying, flung the cloth over his shoulder and went out the back door, never to be seen again. Apparently, this stranger came looking for the Greek, so when he came into the bar, the Greek knew it was time to split, even though he had been there for many years. It was a great talking matter for weeks and there were rumours that it had something to do with a woman, others said it was a gambling debt, that he was an escaped convict on the run and in hiding in Maun. Whatever it was, it scared the Greek barman to go quickly. Nobody ever saw him again and nobody ever knew why, nor where he went.

When we lived in Kasane we sometimes used the services of a pilot in a very small plane if we wanted to fly anywhere, which wasn't often, but he was available to anyone who wanted his services. This pilot was very, very fat and always wore a beige and brown uniform. He was a very nice man, but it always amused and worried me, as to the fact that he looked heavier than his plane and when we went up in it with him, I was scared stiff that his weight would bring the plane down. The first time we went up with him, he flew us all over the Okavango swamps and over the Victoria Falls, which was a fantastic experience. But then he did something that I didn't find funny at all and that was, turn the plane upside down. I felt the bush come up and hit me between the eyes and vomited my Rhodesian mixed grill upside down, so that it floated all over the place. Not a nice experience at all. This man also lived all by himself, another loner in the bush.

We had some lovely friends who had the curio shop at the Victoria Falls and whenever we went on our shopping trips we would go and visit them and they would come and see us in Kasane and sometimes leave their kids with us for a week or so, so that I had company to play with. One day while they were travelling through the bush, a huge buck with long straight horns came running out of the bush and ran straight at the car. One of its horns went through the windscreen, pierced the woman's forehead and came out at the back of her head, killing her instantly. It shocked us all terribly, as it was such a freak accident and so sudden. Her husband sold his shop and disappeared from our lives and we never knew what happened to him but heard that he was never the same after that.

There were Scottish and Anglican missions, where, apart from the permanent members, there were constant visitors from sister missions in the UK that would come out for the experience and we kids would laugh at them because they seemed so green and didn't know what anything was about. I look back now and realise that those young people had probably never left their cosy home towns before coming out to the bush. But we were hardened bush kids by this time and had no time for softies.

There was also a trickle of writers and film-makers who passed through from time to time. They would come out to write books, make documentaries or films about the Bushmen, the bush or the animals. One lady came out to write about the Okavango and she and her husband stayed on a houseboat with retractable wheels so it could travel overland too. She would come into the village and mix with the locals, both black and white, asking everyone a lot of questions and jotting things down. She always wore khaki and red lipstick and would swan around as though she were the Queen of Africa, which is what the white women called her. She had a very haughty attitude that made people uncomfortable around her. One day Aggie baked a large batch of fresh bread, so Mum asked the "Queen of Africa" if she would like some fresh bread. This lady looked down her nose at Mum and said, "yes please, I'll have one white, one wholewheat and two seed loaves please".

You could have knocked down Mum with a feather.

"In that case, you'll have nothing," she said, and turned and walked away from the woman. Mum had offered what we had but we were not a shop. You couldn't buy bread in the bush at that time, so I could understand Mum's attitude. Later on, when this woman's book was published and we were sent a copy by my grandmother in England, the white community were incensed by the things she had written about them, calling them 'leather skinned savages'.

One day an American millionaire came wandering into Dad's office and said that he had come out to photograph the Kalahari and where could he stay? As there were no hotels where we were living, Dad said that he could stay with us, so Mum put him up in the guest room and he had his meals with us. The next day he asked Dad to take him into the Kalahari and Dad told him that he was already there. But the old fellow insisted that he wanted to be shown to the Kalahari and Dad, becoming fed up with the old man's timewasting, took him by the arm and said, "so you want me to take you to the Kalahari desert, do you?" The American said yes, that was what he had been asking all along. Dad took him by the arm and walked to the border of our yard, opened the gate and said, "now you are in the Kalahari desert". Eventually the old man got the idea and took some great photos, which he sent us, together with a lovely thank-you letter, when he got back to the States.

There were a lot of Afrikaans farmers scattered all over the B.P. and they were a hardened lot, salted by generations of hard life in the bush since the great trek and had the land in their blood. They were very generous to us whenever we visited them but they lived in a world so different to us, a world that only they belonged to and which, at times, I envied. I envied their stability, their roots, their belonging to generations of volk that had done the same as they were doing now.

There were also people who had 'gone native' or *kaffir*, as was said in those awful days. These were people who were trying to break with convention, tradition, unhappy family lives, debt, disillusion, or just wanted to get back in touch with nature. These people were usually intelligent folk, quiet and well spoken, usually men, who would take native wives, adopt the native culture and have nothing to do with the outside world at all.

Then there were the drifters who would come by. They would appear out of nowhere and disappear again into nowhere. Nobody knew what they were doing there in the bush and nobody really cared. In those days, the BP wasn't a tourist place where people went for holidays, not even safaris. Not many people even knew where it was. Today it is overrun with tourists looking for exotic holidays and I am thankful that I was lucky enough to know it when it was still relatively wild and unspoilt.

# 7.  Molepolole

I have recently read that Molepolole[6] is the world's largest village, I don't know whether that is true or not and I really don't know how they judge these things. My husband says that Madrid is the biggest village in the world, because it has always been classified as a village, so I suppose we could all claim something different and think that we were right. I do remember Molepolole as being a large dust village that sprawled out into a dust bowl that could be seen from our house. We weren't part of the village, we were apart from the village, observing from a safe distance. Again, we had the typical government house, with the veranda running around the whole house, encased by the green mosquito netting and red polished floors. Again we had the big yard and higgledy-piggledy garden made up of anything that survived the heat. We had the flagpole with the union jack, saluted up at sunrise and saluted down at sunset. This house was different in that it had two *rondavels* off the main house. These little round mud huts with their thatched roofs humming with wildlife were converted by my mother into a guest room and a dining room. I loved these huts because they felt secure, cool and quiet. I would take refuge in the guest room during the heat of the day and play all by myself, imagining myself to be living on an island.

---

[6] Molepolole lies in the south-east of the country, 50 kilometres west of the capital Gaborone and acts as gateway for exploring the Kalahari desert. Molepolole serves as the capital of the Bakwena, one of the three major tribes in Botswana, who make up the majority of its residents. It is named after the Molepolole river. It is Botswana's biggest village and one of the largest traditional villages in Africa, with a population of 69,789 people as of 2008. It has a large traditional court (or *kgotla*) and is the location of the Scottish Livingstone Hospital, one of the nation's largest.

I was still at boarding school when we lived in Molepolole and I didn't spend too much time at home, so I have faded memories about our time there. I remember it being a dull place at the time, no river and no kids to play with, although we did do trips with Dad into the bush, calling in on the farms and villages, which I enjoyed. It is also said that the first school and the first church in Botswana were built in Molepolole, but I can't vouch for these details.

I do remember that there were two missions there, the Livingstone Scottish Mission, run by a very fine doctor and his staff. No finer man could you find in Africa, he was a saint to everyone he came in contact with. I remember at Christmas they put on a living nativity show, with all the little picaninnies taking part and it was so poignant and moving, especially when they sang their hymns and Christmas carols.

Then there was the Anglican Mission, which was run by a strange priest and his even stranger wife, who had a haircut like a pudding bowl. One day the few white women who lived in the vicinity had a Tupperware party because there was a travelling saleswoman passing through. This was going to be a grand day because not much happened unless there were visitors passing through or official visitors, when there would be a party in their honour.

All the women involved in the Tupperware party had baked cakes galore and were having a grand old time, whooping it up and gorging on cake, when a messenger arrived at the back door, asking to speak to the Anglican minister's wife. She got up and went to see what he wanted and when she came back into the room, she sat down, ashen-faced and very quiet. When the hostess asked her what the matter was, she said that her husband had dropped dead an hour ago. All the women bustled around her, pouring her hot cups of sweet tea for the shock. It was suggested that the party should end and that everyone should go with the poor lady to the mission to see if they could help in any way but the minister's wife thought otherwise.

"No my dears," she declared. "The show must go on! Teddy always loved a good Tupperware party. He's dead now and there's nothing that can be done about it, so let's all have some fun!"

So the party went on, although the rest of the women were rather subdued after that. I cannot hear of Tupperware without thinking of this incident in Molepolole.

Because of the missions in the village, there were always visiting religious students and church people turning up from time to time, which broke the monotony. Apart from the missions, a few white folk filled various posts in the area, which at least gave Mum and Dad a bit of company. I look back now and think of Mum in some of these posts where there was nothing, no neighbours, no shops, no telly nor radio. Mum wasn't a person who baked or sewed and she had the servants looking after the house and garden. I think she must have gone mad at times and I wished I had had the opportunity to talk to her about it.

Gaborone, the capital, wasn't far from Molepolole and we would go into the big town sometimes when Dad had business to see to there and it meant a lunch out at the hotel, shopping and even some English books could be found there.

The missionary David Livingstone had spent some time in the area when he was in Africa and there were some caves near Molepolole called Kobokwe Caves, known also as Livingstone's Caves. Local legend had it that these caves were inhabited by evil spirits and that anyone who visited them was doomed never to return. In an effort to disprove this myth, David Livingstone apparently spent a night in them, together with a local king called Kgosi Sechele, in an effort to convert the king and the locals to Christianity by proving that there were no evil spirits there. That's the story we were told and it could very well be true, but as time goes by, stories change, depending on who tells them and Africa is full of magical tales that change with the winds of time. But Livingstone was certainly in the area and the caves are named after him, so it is likely that the story is true.

We would sometimes go for picnics in the area where the caves were, because there were some lovely shady trees and a dried up old river bed that had lovely white sand like a beach, but without the water. The adults would sit around drinking under the trees and have a barbecue while us kids would play in the river bed, which was a real treasure trove. Just under the surface of the sand there were thousands of different coloured, semi-precious stones, agates, tigers eye, red jasper, turquoise, jade, quartz of various colours and a lot more that I don't know the names of. We would fill buckets with these stones and take them home with us. Today these treasures would fetch a fortune but we just wanted them for the pretty colours and even the adults didn't take much notice of them. We would also climb up into the caves where it was cool and the walls were etched with ancient Bushman drawings and our voices would echo off the cave walls that had seen life pass through many aeons. Today I'm sure we wouldn't be allowed to play there as we did as children, because the importance of conserving these treasures is now recognised.

I can't say much more about our stay in Molepolole. This was the last post we were stationed at before independence. Independence Day was looming and it made quite a lot of white people insecure. Dad was offered a post in the new Botswana and also other posts in other British colonies, but he decided to go back to England. He got a job at Newcastle University, in Newcastle-on-Tyne, which was a dramatic change from Africa but within two years he was restless again and applied for a job in Sierra Leone, which he got.

After Sierra Leone he went to South Africa and another adventure started for us.

# 8. Independence and England

As Independence Day approached, when Bechuanaland Protectorate was to become Botswana on September 30$^{th}$ 1966, the white community became restless. Some were staying on, others were going on to other British colonies or to neighbouring South Africa but most of the British were going back to England. Dad wasn't sure whether it would be wise to stay on in the new country because he said that the future wasn't very clear. Years later, he regretted his decision and wished that he had stayed on, as he had been asked to do.

There were celebrations planned for the big day and I remember the preparations being made in Molepolole. There were going to be a lot of official parades and speeches involving the handing over of the outgoing to the incoming government. Mum was organising women's choral groups, a beauty pageant, a baby show, races of all kinds, games for the kiddies and competitions of various types. The locals were preparing their best clothes for the big day and everyone was preparing food, which would be on sale all around the village for the festivities.

While all this was going on, we were packing up our house into tea chests, trunks and suitcases. The conversation at home was all about what we would do when we got back to England. Dad would have to look for a job, we would have to look for somewhere to live and, worst of all, Tom and I would have to look for new schools. Tom would go to his first school when we got back and I, at the difficult age of thirteen, would have to try to adapt to England in the sixties, after a life in the bush.

I had said a sad farewell to all my friends at boarding school and was extremely sad to be leaving the only life I had known until then and very scared about what awaited me in England.

The 30$^{th}$ September 1966 arrived and, amongst our half-packed luggage, we dressed in our best and went out to celebrate the new Botswana. Dad wore his white official 'ice-cream' suit, Mum wore a navy blue suit and a hat and I don't remember what I wore, but we kids weren't important. Mum and Dad had to attend all the official ceremonies. There were a lot of important dignitaries, both black and white, dressed up in different uniforms and suits, many with rows of medals across their chests. There were celebrations going on all over the country but in Molepolole we celebrated in our own special way. There was a feeling of unity amongst the black and white citizens of the village that was very emotional.

It was a very windy day, which was unfortunate, because the wind whipped up huge dust storms that covered everything in a fine sand and everyone had to close their eyes against the grit getting in. A big fat young lady won the beauty pageant, one of our garden boys came last in the marathon and the baby who won the healthiest and most beautiful baby in the village, died at the end of the day and nobody knew why. This incident upset Mum very much because she was a nurse and also one of the judges and felt that she must have missed something when checking the baby and this spoilt the day for her. It was a very sad end to our stay there.

There were lots of long speeches in both languages, there was a lot of singing and dancing all day and there were oxen roasting on spits and tables laden with food from all cultures, not only European cuisine, the African women had done themselves proud with their local dishes, the Indians produced spicy curries and the Afrikaans community laid on enough food for the Great Trek. The food was fantastic, albeit gritty, but nobody seemed to mind. There was also a lot of drinking going on and a fine time was had by all.

In the evening there was a firework display and the partying went on until the next day, when Bechuanaland Protectorate was officially Botswana and we Brits had to come to terms with the fact that we had to let go. I think the most poignant and saddest moment was when the British Anthem was played and the Union Jack came down for the last time. When the

Botswana anthem played and the new flag was hoisted, there was a great feeling of hope for the future and there wasn't a dry eye in the whole of Molepolole that day. Dad was presented with the last Union Jack to come down and the first Botswana flag to go up. I still have that Botswana flag, but the Union Jack disintegrated, maybe with age, or perhaps an omen.

We left a couple of days after Independence. We said goodbye to friends and neighbours, paid off our servants and bade them farewell and many thanks for their faithful service. They wept and so did we but what hurt me terribly was saying goodbye to Aggie, who had been with us since our arrival in Africa ten years previously and had crossed the country many times just to be with us. She was a mother to me and had seen me grow from tiny tot to teenager and I loved her. She wasn't young when she first came to us and, indeed, didn't know her own age, but she was looking old and tired now and had decided to go back to her village and retire. She said she didn't want to work anymore but, knowing Aggie, she would have gone back to her village and built new huts for her growing family, which now included grandchildren, tended the chickens and goats, ploughed her bit of land, pounded the mielie and looked after her numerous grandchildren. None of that would she consider 'work'. She was tired of serving the white madam and wanted to look after her own business now. I liked to think of her sitting in a home-made wood and cow-hide rocking chair, in front of her mud hut, watching the sun go down beyond the thorn trees, while she puffed on her pipe, which was her one vice, while her brood of children and grandchildren ran around obeying her orders, looking after her, but I know that she was too active at that time to let that happen.

We boarded our last Union Castle liner for our trip back to the UK, not sure what was waiting for us the other end. When we arrived in Southampton it was cold, grey and wet, which didn't do much for our morale. As I mentioned earlier, Dad had got a job at Newcastle University. He had applied for jobs from Botswana and had been informed just before we left that

Newcastle University wanted to interview him, so at least we had a destination to aim for. While we were house-hunting we stayed in the most depressing boarding house you could possibly find. The menu was geared towards the mainly geriatric clientele. Everything was unsalted, tepid and pale in colour, so we didn't know what we were eating. The best thing was the tapioca pudding, because at least it was served with a big dollop of strawberry jam to give it some taste.

Eventually we found a house that was converted into two flats. We rented the bottom flat, which had a garden, while the Jewish owner lived in the top flat.

Tom was put into a good school down the road and although he adapted well to school, probably because at last he had friends to play with, he would not keep his shoes on, even in the snow because he was so used to walking barefoot in the bush. His teachers were always phoning Mum because Tom would think he could still do whatever he did in Africa and he was totally out of control. Dad felt guilty about all my school changes, so he thought he would make it up to me by putting me into a very expensive private school, not far from where we lived. But I was also a bush baby compared to all these young ladies. All the girls in this school were into boys, makeup, the Beatles, the Rolling Stones and fashion, the Twiggy look, Mary Quant, miniskirts, etcetera and there was I, a total nerd, who didn't know what the hell was going on and felt as though I had landed on another planet. My schoolwork wasn't up to scratch either, so I had to have extra classes in almost all subjects, which didn't help much. I didn't fit in, didn't have friends and missed Africa so much it hurt.

This went on for two years until Dad said that he wanted to go back to Africa, so another move was imminent. He couldn't find a job in South Africa, where he wanted to go, but was offered a job in Sierra Leone, which he accepted. The problem was that there weren't any schools in Sierra Leone for girls my age, so I would have to go to another boarding school in South Africa.

I was now fifteen, going on sixteen.

# 9.   Johannesburg

We flew to South Africa, where I was to be found suitable accommodation and to be enrolled into a finishing school, where I would be taught secretarial skills, how to be a perfect lady and an even more perfect hostess. I was enrolled at a college in the centre of Johannesburg and the college gave my parents the address of a family who took in student lodgers. We went to see them and they seemed nice enough. My parents left me with this family while they went up to Botswana to see old friends, then they were due back in a week's time before they flew off to their new life in Sierra Leone. They figured that it would give me a week to settle in and then they could see if I was happy before they left me and off they went.

The family consisted of a mother, father, a teenage daughter and two older teenage sons. I was given a room and shared meals with them. I felt rather abandoned when Mum, Dad and Tommy left me there. It was a Friday and I was to start college on the following Monday, so it gave me a couple of days to get used to my surroundings.

I started classes and felt very much the new girl, not knowing anyone and wished I could have gone to Botswana with the rest of the family, but as my classes were due to start, I had to stay behind. At the family home, I also felt out of it and I think the children of the house made fun of me behind my back. I didn't seem to fit in anywhere. The night before Mum and Dad were due back in Johannesburg, before taking their flight to Sierra Leone, something happened to change the course of events. I had just fallen to sleep when I had the feeling that I was suffocating. I struggled to open my eyes as I awoke and what I saw threw me into a blind panic. The father of the house and his two sons were on top of me and had thrown a huge piece of steak across my face, which was what gave me the suffocating feeling and they were grappling with my nightclothes. This was clearly a case of attempted rape. I tried to kick them off, but they snarled at me, telling me to shut up if I knew what was good for me. I banged on the wall next to my bed, which was the wall separating the parents room from mine. When I did this, the three men jumped off me and ran into the passage. They knew that my banging would alert the mother of the house, which it did. She came into my room to find me gasping and sobbing and she asked me what had happened. When I told her, she laughed and said that I was talking nonsense and that it was all just a nasty dream. The steak wasn't in evidence either, because one of the men had grabbed it as they fled.

The next morning I went to class as if nothing had happened, longing for Mum and Dad to arrive. They turned up at the college before classes were over at midday and I flew into their arms, sobbing my eyes out. When I told them what had happened, Dad spoke to the head of the college who had recommended this family. They said they would look into it and would find me another place to stay in the meantime. But Mum wasn't having any of that. She and Dad booked me a seat on their flight to Sierra Leone later that day. When we went to pick up my things, none of the men were in and nor was the mother. Only the teenage daughter was there and she didn't understand why I was leaving in such a hurry, nor why my Mum was so upset. She obviously didn't know of the previous night's activities.

The big problem was, "what are we going to do about Sue now?" They decided to home school me once we settled into our new home.

# 10.  Sierra Leone

Freetown, the capital of Sierra Leone, to me was beautiful. I loved the colour and the bustle, the sheer exoticness of it. We were allocated a house in a safe compound with other white people. Sierra Leone was known for its corruption, so we were warned of the do's and don'ts of living there. Dad started his new job, Tom was put into an international school and Mum played lady. I was supposed to do lessons at home, but I had no real help and no discipline. We became members of the golf and yacht club, where we made new friends.

I had lost a lot of weight by this time and didn't realise that I was going through anorexia and bulimia, but at least I wasn't a fat slob from the bush anymore. Mum kept saying how beautiful I was, which spurred me on. I had a lot of boyfriends of different ages, nearly all a lot older than me and of a lot of different nationalities. There were people from all over the world in Freetown. There was also a shortage of women, so we girls had the pick of the bunch. The problem was that the pick of the bunch were real men and my friends and I were just little girls playing the role of women. I learned to smoke, drink and flirt like a little tart and Mum and Dad were none the wiser. There were beach parties, yacht parties and exotic restaurants, sailing to nearby islands for parties, speed-boats, casinos and lots of diplomatic parties.

One night I was beaten up by the local police, just for being on the beach after midnight. I didn't know it was forbidden to be on the beach at that time of night but the police didn't listen to me. The next day Dad spoke to an important judge, who was a friend of his, about the situation and the case was dropped, so I didn't have to go to court. The police there were very corrupt and one didn't mess around with them.

Mum being the person she was, and wanting the very best for her daughter, tried very hard to marry me off to a man twice my age who was related to royalty and quite well known. I wasn't interested at all but this poor man fell head-over-heels in love with me and, between him and Mum, they did all sorts of things to try to get me to agree to go to Paris with him. He picked me up and tried to bundle me onto his private jet and whisk me away but I kicked and ranted until he gave up. I heard that he went into a deep depression for a long time after that and Mum was very disappointed in me because she really wanted a daughter with a title.

My parents felt I was getting out of hand because I was at a loose end as to what to do with my time and was always out partying, so the time had come to do something with me. It was decided that I would have to go to boarding school again. Dad contacted a supposed friend of his, in Pretoria in South Africa and asked his advice. This man, Jan, said that there was a very good commercial college in Pretoria that had boarding facilities too. He also said that he and his wife would take me in during the shorter holidays.

So we got on a plane and I headed back to South Africa. We had to be very secretive about my leaving Sierra Leone to go to South Africa because South Africa was still in the thick of apartheid and there was supposed to be no contact between Sierra Leone and South Africa at all. If it was suspected that you had contact with South Africa, you could be locked up as a traitor, so our plans had to be lied about. We said I was en route to the UK.

# 11.  Pretoria

When we got to Pretoria we stayed at Jan's home with his enormous wife and seven children. It was a hot day and the whole of Pretoria was bathed in jacaranda blossoms, which left beautiful lilac carpets of fallen petals everywhere we walked, a truly magnificent sight. Jan's home was big and sprawling, which was necessary with so many children. They were a staunch Afrikaans family, very much in favour of apartheid, just as their ancestors before them had been. I don't remember how Mum and Dad had become friends with them, but it was one of those contacts made years before. Jan was a tiny sinewy man who smoked a pipe and was dwarfed by his enormous wife, who ruled the roost and the kitchen too, making huge six course meals, three times a day. He was a professor at the university in Pretoria.

We went to the commercial school to enrol me and they said that they could admit me straight away, so once again, kitted out in a very dour uniform, I entered the cloisters of a strict Afrikaans boarding establishment, leaving behind the bikinis, miniskirts and palm-fringed beaches. There were English commercial schools in Pretoria but on Jan's advice and my parents anguish about my lack of discipline, they all decided that it was for my best.

I was English and didn't speak Afrikaans. I was surrounded by big Afrikaans girls who, with the exception of a couple of them, came from farming stock and were almost all engaged to be married when they had done their matric, combining their engagement parties with the matric dance. From there they would go on to be good farm wives.

Again, as always, I didn't fit in. I was small in stature, unlike the rest of the girls, I didn't speak their lingo and I had just come from living the life of a high-society jet-setter, which these girls couldn't even imagine. I had left the sports cars and yachts behind and had now got to get used to stodgy food, hard maths and bookkeeping. What a change it all was.

I felt that my parents had abandoned me again and at an age where I was a woman, not a child to be punished for talking after lights out. The new girls were put through some very cruel initiation ceremonies and I was no exception. We had to scale up a date palm with our bare legs and pick every date that grew at the top of the tree, coming down a bleeding mess. We were made to go into town dressed like babies and try to pick up passing men and one girl was buried alive and then brought up out of the makeshift grave just before she passed out. This sort of thing was rife in South Africa at the time and every now and then you would read in the press of kids dying in some awful initiation ceremony.

All the girls at this school had a lot in common so they bonded, while I was the onlooker and I felt like a trespasser. I had grown up while in Sierra Leone and while all these Afrikaans girls were much bigger than I and already engaged to be married, I felt far more mature and sophisticated than them.

I had no inclination to study, I was bored, lonely and depressed and I paid no attention in class. At night I would get out of the window in my room and wander off by myself, just to get away from the stifling four walls. A couple of times I was caught and brought back to face the hostel master, who would give me a telling off and punish me by not letting me go to the cinema with the other girls on Saturday. He said that he wasn't going to punish me too severely because he understood that I was far from home and my situation was out of the ordinary. Too true it was out of the ordinary!

When the holidays came round, the girls would take turns in inviting me to go home with them, because it was too far for me to go back to Sierra Leone. But although these girls were being kind, once I got to their homes, usually big Afrikaans farms, I would feel awkward and so would they and their families. Most of them found English difficult and I didn't speak Afrikaans and we had nothing in common. There came a time when the hostel master would say, "who is going to take Susan this time?" to which they would reply "we took her last holiday" or "we can't this time because we are going to our grandma's house at the coast". There were always excuses and it always hurt like hell.

At the beginning of the term, I went to stay with Jan and his family, as agreed by his family and my parents. After all, they were also to administer my pocket money, which Dad had left Jan in charge of. One day I was waiting by the gate with my suitcase all packed, for a long weekend. Jan was supposed to pick me up. I was still waiting hours later, after all the others had been picked up by their parents. In the end I had to go back into the hostel and spend the weekend by myself. This brought back memories of being left at the convent in Mafeking when I was younger, because my parents had forgotten to collect me. Some things hadn't changed.

Jan and his wife had moved to another town, selling their house and taking my meagre pocket money with them. They hadn't notified my parents or the school and, least of all, me. I was left with no money and nowhere to go. To top it all, I had heard on the news that there was an uprising in Sierra Leone. I wrote home but got no reply at all, just silence. This silence went on for months and I didn't know what had happened to my family.

One day I was in bookkeeping class, my least favourite class, when a prefect came in and told the teacher that the headmaster wanted to see me in his office. I was being summoned and I didn't know what I had done wrong. I followed the prefect down the corridor, asking her if she knew what it was all about. She said that she didn't, but added, "have you been up to your tricks again meisie?" I felt like slapping the sly grin off her face but thought better of it as we approached the dreaded door. I knocked and heard the headmaster say "kom in", so I pushed the door open slowly but when I went into the office I started feeling faint, the whole room started moving around me and I started sweating. There, sitting in front of the big desk, were my family, Mum, Dad and Tom. I just stood there, not knowing what to say, I was numb. Mum rushed up and hugged me, followed by a chaste kiss from Dad. Little Tommy was shy and embarrassed by the whole episode. I felt cold.

The headmaster told me that my parents had come to collect me earlier than the school closed because they wanted to take me to Durban, where we were going to live. As all the exams were finished, there was no need to stay on. He said that I could collect my report at the beginning of the next year, which was a month away, but if I wanted to know the results I could phone in a week's time. I didn't want to go with my parents but I didn't want to stay there either. I was a total mental wreck. When my family started to move towards the door, I clung onto the chair trembling and crying, I didn't want to go with them, I didn't want another start in another town, I had had enough. I had had enough of travelling, of different schools, of different towns, different countries, enough of everything.

# 12.  Durban

Before coming to collect me in Pretoria, my parents had gone to Durban and Dad had found an administrative job. They also bought the first house they had ever owned. The house was beautiful, with lovely views over Durban, but there was a snag; it was in a new area in Westville, far from anywhere. Mum didn't drive and Dad had the only car. Tommy went to school on a bicycle. It was a problem to go to the beach or the shops and we had to wait until Dad was free.

Another problem was that nobody knew what to do with me. I refused to go to another school and I also refused to phone my old school in Pretoria to ask for my exam results because I knew what the outcome would be. I hadn't taken the slightest interest in schoolwork the previous year, so I just didn't care.

One day I saw an ad in the local newspaper for beauty courses, so I thought that would be just up my street and Mum and Dad enrolled me. The course was in a small beauty salon on the marine parade in the centre of Durban, which meant that I had to go in with Dad in the mornings and wait for him to bring me back in the evenings. I quite enjoyed the course, as it was very hands-on, with a lot of practical work besides all the theory that we had to learn, but at last I didn't feel like a child anymore.

On my lunch hour I would go to the beach and eventually became one of the surfing crowd. I also made friends with the other girls doing the course, which was really good for me.

When my parents and Tom had left Sierra Leone, they travelled by a Dutch cargo ship down the west coast of Africa to Durban. They had made good friends with the first officer, a Dutchman from The Hague, called Henk. One day this man phoned Mum and Dad, saying that his ship was in port and he would like to see them, so Mum invited him to our house for supper. That night, I fell in love, truly and madly. I had had lots of boyfriends of all nationalities and ages while in Sierra Leone, but nothing serious, they were just childhood loves, but this was different. Henk was short, dark, corpulent and with the bluest eyes I had ever seen and he was also nearly twenty years older than me. The best part of all this was that he felt the same way about me and my parents were also delighted at the liaison.

After that night, whenever Henk's ship was in port he would visit me and during his trips he would phone me whenever his ship called in at a port. He would send flowers and gifts from many exotic locations and I was the happiest girl alive.

One day Dad came home and said that the company he worked for had closed down, just like that, without any warning, so he was out of a job. We were short of money at the time because of the hefty mortgage, so things were a bit strained. Eventually, after many weeks of job hunting, Dad took a job selling houses for a local estate agent. This wasn't what he wanted to do and he became very miserable indeed. Dad wasn't a good salesman and wasn't selling any houses. Eventually he found an administrative job at Wits University in Johannesburg.

When my parents told me that we were moving to Jo'burg, I was furious. What would happen to my beauty course? I was only half way through it. And what would happen to my relationship with Henk? He couldn't come into port in Jo'burg could he? There was no bloody sea there! I ranted to my parents. I refused to move. We eventually came to an agreement. They said that I could come to Durban every time Henk was in port and also take my beauty exams. I spoke to my tutor, who wasn't very happy about the situation but there was nothing I could do. I knew that I would miss out on a lot of the practical work and would have to do more theory to make up for it.

The house was sold and our little rescue dog, Chips, was left with our neighbours until we settled down in Jo'burg, when we would come back and collect him.

So off we went on another adventure.

# 13.   Johannesburg, Durban ... and Back

When we got to Johannesburg we were allocated a flat in a complex of old converted houses in a lovely area in Parktown. The old house was lovely but I had to share a bedroom with Tommy, which wasn't so good after having a lovely bedroom to myself in Durban.

Dad settled down and was happy in his new job and Mum was offered the job of caretaker of the university flats in return for a free flat, maid service, telephone bills and gardener.

I didn't have any friends in Johannesburg, so I felt that once more I was alone. I went back and forth to Durban whenever Henk came into port but it started to get me down and I went into a deep depression. I went to see my doctor in Durban, who prescribed an antidepressant, which made me behave as though I was a raving lunatic. When Henk came into port he thought I was high on drugs and I received a letter from him when I was back in Jo'burg, explaining that he wanted to break off our relationship because he didn't want to marry a drug addict. In the meantime, I went back to my doctor and they found out that I was allergic to these pills. I wrote and told Henk but he said he needed time, because he wasn't sure whether I was telling him the truth.

I returned to Durban to do my final exam and got my diploma. I worked in a salon there for a while but wasn't happy and I decided that from now on there was no reason to return to Durban and I had decided to try and make a life for myself in the city of gold.

I couldn't find a job in a beauty salon so I took a job in a hairdressing salon doing manicures and manning the reception desk. This little salon was in the heart of Hillbrow, a bus ride away from Parktown. I loved my job and my boss and was relatively happy. Although I was fairly content, I needed more money that my boss wasn't willing to pay, so I found another job in the centre of Jo'burg in an employment agency.

While I was at this job I met a man who had a flat and business on the floor above my office, a German called Hal. Hal was an astrologist and faith healer. He was tall and blonde with blue eyes. I was drawn to him, more because I was interested in his work than in the man himself. Eventually we started dating and within six months we were married, a big white wedding in the spiritualist church in the centre of town, with a big ceremony in Mum and Dad's garden. This was the wedding Mum had dreamed of: white dress, marquee, caterers, guests from all over the world, the lot. There was only one fly in the ointment; I didn't love my new husband, I was still in love with my Dutchman.

Hal and I worked the four health centres he owned, between Johannesburg, Pretoria and Durban, so we were kept busy, but we weren't happy. I was, by this time, getting a lot of physical and mental abuse, so I decided to leave and sue for divorce. Our marriage had lasted seven months. I walked away from my husband with only a divorce certificate under my arm and nothing else, but I felt so free.

While Hal and I had been running the businesses I had also got a job as caretaker in a big block of flats in Hillbrow, close to one of our clinics because we got a free flat which was a great help, because although business was steady, our overheads were steep and we were just keeping afloat. When we separated, Hal had to move out because the flat came with my job. I felt that I couldn't stay on in the job though, because it was too close to the clinic and I wanted to get away from Hal. I got a job in the Carlton hotel in Jo'burg, in the housekeeping department, which was fine to start off with, but when I found that I was being stalked by my ex-husband I decided to leave and go back to Durban.

Mum had also dropped a bombshell at this time; she told me that a letter had arrived from Henk on the morning of my wedding to Hal. She had opened it and read it. In the letter he had said that he was sorry about everything and wanted to make up again. Mum thought it better not to upset the perfect wedding and had thrown the letter away. By the time she had told me this, it was too late. I wrote to Henk and explained everything, telling him that I had married on the rebound and that I had only just found out about his letter and that now I was single. I got a letter back saying that as he hadn't heard from me, he had married the first woman who had come along and was expecting twins any day.

I found a job in the Edward hotel on the beach front of Durban's golden mile and left immediately by train. It was 24th December, Christmas Eve, and Durban was heaving with summer holidaymakers. When I got there in the evening, I tried finding accommodation for the night, until I could find something more permanent. The more I trudged the streets, the darker it got and the more desperate I felt. Eventually I stumbled into a small, dingy looking place, with a very painted thin lady behind the reception. I told her that I was looking for a room but she said that I couldn't stay there because it wasn't the sort of place for someone like me. I told her I was desperate for somewhere for the night. Anyway, she relented and gave me a room. I was exhausted and fell into a deep sleep.

The next day I went to the hotel where they explained all the ins and outs of my job as executive housekeeper and said that I could start the next day, Christmas day. It was a very lonely Christmas, but at least I was away from that monster.

After work that day I went back to my dingy little room and fell asleep, trying to block out the sounds of uninvited festivities. In the middle of the night, my door was flung open and there in front of my bed were three policemen with guns. Behind the policemen was the thin painted lady from behind the reception desk and she was saying, "leave her alone, she's not one of them, she's only staying here because she hasn't anywhere else to stay". The policemen turned around and left the room and I fell asleep again, totally exhausted.

It turned out that I was in a whorehouse and didn't know it. I stayed on in that whorehouse because it was convenient and came to love the girls and their thin, painted madame. They protected me, gave me lots of advice about men and their customers were told to leave me alone. Some of the favourites would bring me gifts and treated me like a little sister. Every time the police raided, they knew to leave me alone. I settled down into my new job and was looking around for a more suitable place to live when the bottom fell out of my world once again. I was coming out of the hotel after a busy day at work and there, right in front of the hotel, was my ex-husband's car, with him sitting behind the wheel. I asked the doorman how long the car had been there and he said that it was there with the same man behind the wheel for the last couple of days. I noticed that he was looking the other way, so he didn't see me and I went back into the hotel and left via the back door. The next day I told my boss that I was leaving my job to go back to Jo'burg. I was being stalked again and I wanted to be close to my family while this was going on. I also found out that he had got a private detective following me around too, so I didn't want to stay around.

Back in Johannesburg, I found a lovely job in a big residential hotel in Hillbrow, working as receptionist/housekeeper. I was given a lovely room and all meals, laundry and phone calls paid for. The stalking stopped from then on and I was happy. I started dating again and made new friends. I didn't live too far from Mum and Dad either, so I would see them as often as I wanted, but had my own space.

It was at this hotel where I met Carlos, my present husband. He was a Spaniard working with a Spanish firm in Jo'burg and was living in the hotel where I was working. It was hotel policy not to go out with hotel guests, so we had to meet in secret. Carlos didn't speak English and I didn't speak Spanish, but it made no difference at all. When he went back to Spain, I followed a few months later.

I loved Carlos but I didn't love Spain, so I decided to go back to South Africa after three months. I said a tearful farewell to Carlos and headed back. I found a job in a lovely country hotel on the outskirts of Rivonia and although I was happy there, I missed Carlos a lot and he missed me too, so we used to phone each other every day. I began to feel sick too and it wasn't long before the doctor confirmed that I was pregnant. Carlos phoned me on my birthday, which also happens to be his birthday, and I told him that he was going to be a father. His reaction was, "I am going to send you a ticket tomorrow and you are coming back to Spain where I can look after you."

I toyed with the idea because I loved Carlos a lot and he loved me but I detested his country and I didn't know what to do for the best. After a lot of thinking and not very much sleeping, I decided that if we loved each other we had a good base from which to start, especially for a baby that really needs that love and I was sure that the rest would follow. Carlos couldn't come back to South Africa at the time because he had recently opened a business with a friend, so he had a lot to lose. The trouble was that I couldn't leave straight away because we were barricaded in the hotel due to rioting in the townships around the area where the hotel was situated. South Africa was still in the horrible apartheid era and was going through some of the worst times it had ever seen. When things quietened down a bit, I got on a plane and went back to Madrid where Carlos was waiting for me with open arms.

# 14.   Spain

Just after I arrived in Spain, Carlos's business folded, due to lack of customers and a spendthrift partner, so we had to look elsewhere. In the meantime we were living with his parents in the centre of Madrid, which wasn't the most congenial situation for anyone. There was still the language barrier, not only between Carlos and I , but also between his family and I. They thought I was really very strange. The Spain of then cannot be compared with the Spain of today. Today it is a thriving, modern, democratic country, but at that time, it was still trying so hard to find itself after Franco's death and it was stuck in a time warp compared to many modern countries, South Africa included. Not speaking Spanish and being pregnant, meant that finding a job was impossible, so it was all up to Carlos. Eventually, he found a job in a little village called Reinosa, up north, in Cantabria, not far from Santander. We said adios to his family and boarded a train north. We arrived at Reinosa station near midnight, in the thick of winter. Carlos had been to the village beforehand and had found us a flat, so we went straight there by taxi and fell into bed. Our flat was wooden, wooden, floors, ceilings, windows, doors, wall panels; everything was wooden, old and creaking. We had a little balcony that I was afraid to stand on, in case it collapsed under me, but the views were magnificent. Later on, we moved twice more while living in Reinosa, but no matter where we lived, the views were lovely. It was a large rural community, surrounded by mountains, fields, streams and contented cows dotted on the landscapes. The sunrises and sunsets were some of the best I have seen anywhere in the world. But life was hard. Carlos would go to work early in the dark snowy mornings and I would be left on my own all day, with no telly, radio, books or friends and nobody who understood English and heavily pregnant to boot.

We didn't have any money at that time, so we couldn't do much more than go for long walks in the country. I had no washing machine either, so all our washing had to be done bent over the bath tub and then hung on a line strung from the kitchen window, where I would bring it in at the end of the day, frozen solid. We had the flat strewn permanently with wet washing in front of heaters, which gave off a fuggy steam. Oh how I missed Africa. Being a child, product, or victim, depending on how you look at it, of colonialism, I didn't know the first thing about keeping house. I couldn't cook, couldn't clean, nor wash, nor iron. I had never been taught. I had always had servants to do it all for me. Even in Africa we never had a washing machine in those days, we still had a Joanna, a Beauty, or whatever the maids were called, who did it all for us. I was totally at sea and felt completely and utterly lost.

My mother in law thought I was the most useless creature she had ever clapped eyes on and cursed the day her son had brought me to Spain. Spanish housewives lived for housework and cooking and looking after their children and prided themselves on their duties. I used to go out at eight in the morning with my shopping bag, not realising that they don't open their shops until ten or after and the curtains of the houses in the village would twitch as I walked down the street and I could feel invisible eyes following me down those cold cobbled streets.

I was a vegetarian at the time and protein substitutes in Spain were non-existent. There were no supermarkets as there are today, so I would have to go to the local market and actually ask for what I wanted, which I didn't know the names of. I would stand in queues for ages just for a couple of carrots and not understand how I never seemed to get closer to the counter, but it was because all these big fat country Marias would barge in front of me and I wouldn't know how to say, "hey, it's my turn", or whatever. I would go home in tears with a whole feathered chicken and not know what to do with the thing. You would have thought that life in the bush had prepared me for this situation, but alas no, simply because, the servants had seen to all this sort of thing. When I did learn the name of a new food, we would eat it every day until we were sick of the sight and taste of it and then I would have to I learn another word.

I would go off to the local doctor for my prenatal check-ups and he prodded me and took blood from me and mumbled things to me that I didn't understand. I had a very strange craving while pregnant and that was for *sol y sombra*, which translated means, "sun and shadow." It is a drink of a tot of anise, topped with a tot of brandy. Now, I have never been a big drinker, but I craved this stuff, so I would go to the bar beneath our flat and ask for my favourite tipple for breakfast, together with a thick hot chocolate, so thick the teaspoon would stand up in it and a plate full of *churros*, those crispy, deep fried bits of dough, sprinkled with sugar. Not the healthiest of breakfasts, especially while pregnant, but at least it kept the below zero temperatures at bay. I hate to think what the people in the bar thought of this heavily pregnant woman from foreign parts. This part of Spain isn't a typical tourist area, so I was a novelty of sorts.

Towards the end of my pregnancy, I became ill with pre-eclampsia but I didn't know. The doctor told Carlos but Carlos didn't know how to tell me. I knew nothing about pregnancies, nor babies. The worst thing of all was that I had nobody to ask, no support at all. I just knew that I didn't feel very well, but thought that all pregnant women felt the same and all the babbling that went on between the doctor and Carlos didn't make sense to me at all. I was exasperated and so were Carlos and the doctor, who couldn't make me understand what was going on with me. My parents in Johannesburg didn't know what was going on either. Carlos couldn't tell them in his Spanish, I didn't know and we didn't have a phone in the flat. I had to use a public phone booth, which worked sometimes if you were lucky, but more times than not, all it did was swallow all your change, which we could ill afford at that time and without being able to say a word to whomever you phoned.

When I went into labour, it lasted three days and the doctor was telling me to push all the time and then at the end of the three days, he decided that the baby was a breech. They managed to turn the baby at the last moment, which they should have done in the beginning and Ivan was born with the help of forceps and I was finished. But, the baby survived and so did I. Ivan was a beautiful baby, but I was so afraid of him. I hadn't had much to do with babies and my mother hadn't shown me much either, so I had very little to pass onto this new born in my arms. He had a lot of breathing problems and had to be rushed several times into emergency to be revived, but he came through and was a good and happy little fellow. My mother-in –law came from Madrid to help out and she did nothing but criticize everything I did. She had four children of her own, so she obviously had more experience than me, but instinctively I knew that some of the things she said and did, as far as Ivan were concerned, belonged to the ark and I was glad when she left, so that I could muddle along by myself. Carlos was a brilliant father and an even better mother than me. When he was growing up, he had had to help his mother with his younger siblings while his mother was out making a living, so he had a way with babies that I never had. I loved my little Ivan to distraction, but I felt a huge responsibility for him and I didn't feel as though I knew how to look after him. I know now that a lot of new young mothers feel that, but there was nobody to tell me that at the time. I went into a deep depression and had to be treated for it. Two months after Ivan was born, I had terrible cramps and the doctor came out at two in the morning and said that I would have to have my appendix out straight away, so I was whipped in for an emergency operation. When they opened me up, they realised that my appendix was perfectly healthy. I had had a bad reaction to the contraceptive pill that they had put me onto. We could ill afford the expense at the time, because I wasn't on the national health and we had just paid the bills for Ivan's birth. We were just scraping through, when Carlos had a nasty accident at work. He had almost severed his finger and gangrene had set in due to it not being treated properly, by the same doctor who took my appendix out. Carlos was almost unconscious at home and I was on my own with my depression and a new baby. I tried to phone my in-laws to tell them that we would be coming back to Madrid as soon as Carlos could travel, so that he could have specialised treatment. I was lucky that Carlos's younger brother answered the phone that day, because he could understand a bit of broken English. I also phoned Mum in tears and she said that they were sending me tickets to come back to South Africa and they had a friend who offered Carlos a job. This news was the best I had had in my life.

We went to Madrid where Carlos had treatment, but we had to delay our trip to South Africa because Carlos wasn't responding to treatment and living with in-laws with a sick husband and a new baby wasn't fun at all. Eventually the great day arrived and we got on a plane for Johannesburg, Carlos still bandaged up, Ivan nine months old and me, the happiest I had ever been.

# 15. A Wedding, a Baby, a House and a Business

When we arrived in Johannesburg Mum and Dad were at the airport to meet us and they took us straight to their flat in Parktown. Mum was given permission from the university for us to stay in the flat opposite theirs, at least until it was needed by incoming university staff. It was lovely staying in this worldly old building with the lovely gardens, which included a swimming pool and tennis court. The university staff also cleaned our flat for us, which was a sheer luxury after my experience in Spain. I had forgotten how pampered I had been while growing up.

Ivan was made a great fuss over, being the first and only grandchild and it was lovely just to be able to talk in my own language again. Carlos started at his new job and loved it from the start. We bought a second hand car so that he could get to work and we started looking around for a flat to rent in a nice area.

About four days after arriving in Johannesburg, we got married at the Johannesburg registry office. It was a very simple affaire. I bought an off-white, off the shoulder dress in the sales and we took Mum and a couple of our friends from earlier days as witnesses. We hadn't got married in Spain because I was a divorcee and the Spanish authorities didn't recognise divorce, being a catholic country. As it was, our marriage in South Africa was legal, but not in Spain, so while all our documents stated that we were married, Carlo's passport stated that he was single. If he had wanted to marry another woman he could have and wouldn't be labelled a bigamist, at least by the Spanish government. All this made me feel rather insecure.

We found a lovely flat in Bedforview, which was the other side of Jo'burg from where we were staying with Mum and Dad. Firstly we moved into small flat and then into a bigger one when I fell pregnant again. We bought a job lot of second hand furniture from a Cuban friend of ours, who was leaving the country. It was very good quality stuff and was a great bargain. At least our home was taking shape. In the complex we lived in, there were swimming pools and tennis courts and also two big shopping malls, one across the road from us, with an excellent Pick N Pay supermarket, cinemas, beautiful shops, restaurants and medical facilities. The other one was completed a short while after we arrived and was even bigger and better than the closer one and it was just a five minute walk from our flat. There was also a lovely nursery school across the road, which Ivan went to when he was a little older. Once a week I would take Ivan in a pram on the bus, into the centre of Jo'burg and meet Mum for coffee and then go back to Parktown with her, where we would spend the rest of the day until Carlos picked us up and stayed for supper, before we went back to our flat. I loved this time in my life, because it meant that Mum and I had time together, although, after so many years of being separated in boarding school, sometimes things got a little tense between us. Mum suddenly wanted to play mother and I was now a woman and a mother myself and felt that it was probably too late to be mothered.

I fell pregnant at this time and it was totally different to the first time. This time we had a bit more money, so I could get nice maternity clothes and go to the hairdresser. I also went to pre-natal classes, which wasn't an issue in Spain in those terrible days of pregnancy with Ivan. I would swim and laze in the sun, while the maid did my housework and I lapped it up, really appreciating it all. My pregnancy was easier too. I had none of the problems I had had before. I was looking forward to having Mum around when I gave birth to this baby. There was a fly in the ointment though. When I announced my pregnancy to Mum and Dad, over a glass of champagne to celebrate, they too had an announcement to make. They were leaving South Africa to go back to England. My grandmother was very old and they felt that they should look after her. I thought this very odd, because they had never got on with her and she had lived with us while we were in England before, when we came back from Botswana and there had been continuous fighting, with many hurtful words spoken. As it was, she was now in a very good home, with plenty of money behind her and she didn't really want to be with my parents. You could have knocked me down with a feather, it spoiled the occasion for me. I was going to have this baby alone too. Nevertheless, Mum and Dad went ahead with their plans, they packed up their furniture, sold their car and worst of all, they advertised little Chips, our dog in the local rag. He had been brought from Durban a few years before and had settled down nicely in Johannesburg and now they were getting rid of him again. The number of our beloved pets that we had given to good homes, when we moved on in the past, was beyond counting. Unfortunately I couldn't take him because we were living in a flat where animals were not allowed, although we were looking for a house to buy. But I also had a little boy who had a lot of allergies and pets weren't an option at that stage, although later on we did get dogs, as the children's health improved. I must admit though, Dad did interview a lot of people who answered the advertisement. He insisted that it be a loving family with a garden. In the end, he went to a lovely family with children and a garden, but it still hurt.

Mum and Dad left and we started seriously house hunting, which took up all of our weekends, when Carlos wasn't working. Our baby, another little boy, called Xavier, arrived before we bought a house and this birth was so easy compared to the one before. By this time Ivan had turned three, just two days before his brother's arrival into the world. Unfortunately Xavy was a very sick little baby, he had double pneumonia and was in and out of hospital for quite some time and it was touch and go at times, when we weren't sure if he would make it, but thankfully he did and today is a big strong man nearing thirty.

We bought a lovely single storey, detached house in Germiston, with a pool and lovely garden for the boys to play in. We were very happy and content. I had servants' quarters at the back of the house and employed a lovely woman who helped me with the house and the boys and her husband took care of our garden. We got a rescue dog too, a Labrador-cross who had a nasty habit of escaping and stealing meat from the neighbourhood butcher, so we had to tie her up at night.

Ivan went to a good nursery school in the area until he turned six and Xavy also went there when he turned three. At six, Ivan started at primary school just down our street. Carlos had in the meantime, started a business with some friends of his that he had known for many years.

With the kids now starting schools, we wanted to legalise our situation in Spain. Divorce was still a taboo subject, with the Catholic Church very much holding the reins. I decided to write to the pope and also to the king of Spain, stating my case. I got replies from both of them. The royal house saying that things were about to change in Spain and to be patient. The Vatican saying, that the Catholic cathedral in Johannesburg would contact me to look into the matter. I carried on waiting, but to no avail. I wasn't going to write again. When I had posted these letters, behind the post office counter, there was a very fat, very Afrikaans lady, with spectacles on the end of her nose. And when she saw the addresses of these two letters, she looked up at me over her glasses and asked, "Family?", I nodded the affirmative and she gave me a big grin. Whenever I went into the post office after that, she would treat me like royalty. I didn't think I could go through that again. So just when I decided to give up, I got a phone call from the Catholic Cathedral in Jo'burg, saying that his holiness had contacted them, advising them to get in contact with me. They made an appointment for the next day. When I got to the imposing building the next morning, I was taken into a stark office full of crosses and grim paintings of suffering, where I was interviewed. I told the priest about my case and as I related my tale, the look of distaste spread across his bony face. When I finished my story, he got up and told me that the church would send a priest around to my house, to take more details, so that they could judge whether to continue with the issue or not. I thanked him and held out my hand which he chose to ignore; I was clearly a sinner and a harlot. He did tell me though, that should they continue with my case, they would have to get in contact with my ex-husband, to get his side of the story and that they would want to interview us both together. I told him that that would be impossible, as I was not going to sit in the same room as a wife beater. The whole idea of this was that the Catholic Church wanted to see if there was any viable reason why my first marriage had broken down. They told me that they would see whether there was any way that they could patch up the marriage to make it work. I was flabbergasted. "But I am legally married to another man, a kind, loving, gentle man and we have two children", I said. "I don't want to patch things up with a man that treated me badly, whom I haven't seen in four years and am legally divorced from".

The priest looked over the rims of his glasses and said, "Ah yes, Mrs Hoffmeier (using my ex married surname), but not in the eyes of God". I went home in a daze and told my husband, who went into a state of shock, just as I had. A week later I got another phone call from the Cathedral and they asked whether a priest could come around the next day, so I said it would be alright. I just wanted to see where this would lead.

The next day there was a knock at the door and when I opened the door, it was to find a scruffy, long-haired, bearded fellow, dressed in a pair of jeans, t-shirt and leather sandals, smoking a fag. He introduced himself as Father Whatnot (I cannot remember the name). I invited him in and made us a cup of tea, while he shuffled a lot of papers from a scuffed briefcase. He had also taken a tape recorder out of his case to record our interview. He started asking questions and with every question asked, I felt my jaw drop.

"When your husband brushed his teeth, did he start at the right side of his mouth or the left? When he put his underpants on, did he put his left leg in first, or his right?"

Every question was as banal and ridiculous as the first.

When I asked why all these stupid questions were being asked, I was told it was to judge his character. I was asked about all the gory sexual details of my seven-month marriage. My young brother, who was living with us at the time, was also asked to furnish anything he could about my first marriage. When Tom asked the priest if he really wanted all the details, he was told that they wanted to know everything. So Tom started writing all the details down, page after page, after page and when he finally finished he handed it to the priest, who started reading what Tom had written. As he read down the page, his mouth opened and he just gaped at us, unable to say a word.

"Well you wanted the details, so now you've got them," said Tom and then left the room in disgust.

When the priest finally got up to leave, I asked him, "what about the fact that this man tried to kill me on a daily basis?, that he was abusive?, that he tried to kill my mother?, that he was sleeping around with men and women?, that he was sterile and hadn't told me that he couldn't have children, until after we were married?, are these things not considered sins in the eyes of the Lord and hence, the Catholic church?". I also said, "not once have you asked me about my life now, with my present husband, who is the kindest man and perfect father, nor have you asked about my children and the life we have together now". The priest said that none of that was important, because my life with Carlos didn't exist according to him. The ironic thing was that Carlos was a Catholic, while my first husband belonged to the spiritualist church, where we got married. The spiritualist church doesn't exist in the eyes of the Catholics. The priest left and we heard no more from him, nor the Cathedral for the next four years. In the meantime, I got a phone call one day from the Spanish consulate in Cape Town, telling me to send all our documents like marriage certificate and birth certificates of the whole family, ID cards etc, to them, because divorce in Spain was now legal and so my marriage to Carlos was also legal. At long last it was all over, we were a legal family both in South Africa and in Spain and anywhere else we cared to go in the world. Just before we left South Africa, I got a call from the Catholic Church again, saying that they were now ready to proceed with my case, after investigating circumstances. I told them that it had been four years since I had contacted them and that now it didn't matter, because my marriage was considered legal in Spain's eyes. The priest on the other end of the line said, "that may be so my dear, but it's not legal in the eyes of God". I replied, "I believe in God, father, but where was your God, when my ex-husband was beating me to a pulp?" and I put the phone down, shaking like a mopane leaf on a blustery day.

Carlos had gone into business with a couple of long standing friends and in the beginning it had gone quite well, but things were slowing down and we couldn't afford to plough more money into the business, without selling our house to do it and that wasn't an option for us, so we had to make an important decision. Should we stay in South Africa or go back to Spain?

We toyed with the options. South Africa was in the iron grips of apartheid and it wasn't a happy place to bring children up in. With the problems on the boarders of Angola and Mozambique, the South African army was very active. The call up papers were served on lads of sixteen and those that came back from fighting on the frontiers in one piece physically, were usually scared mentally and we had friends whose son had committed suicide and another who had escaped and was on the run, a deserter after seeing his best friend decapitated, never to live a normal life again. These poor kids, for that's what they were, just kids, had seen such atrocities that they couldn't take anymore. We decided that having two boys, we didn't want that for them. Xavy was just about to turn four and Ivan seven, all this was just around the corner for us. So we sold our house and headed back to Spain. Before leaving the country, we had to get permission for Xavier to leave South Africa. Ivan was alright because like Carlos and I, he had permanent residence and we were not considered South Africans, but Xavy having been born in South Africa, being a male and white, was considered as cannon fodder, as it was known in crude terms. I had to go to the authorities and tell them that we wanted to visit family in Spain for a holiday and they made me sign a document promising to return Xavier to South Africa within a certain time limit, which I did. I felt that once I was out of the country we would be safe. I loved South Africa, but although I had put myself into dangerous situations when I was younger, just to risk having a social life with some of my very good black friends, I couldn't do it on behalf of my little boys, who didn't understand what it was all about. I wanted them growing up knowing that all people are equal, so we knew that our time in South Africa had ended.

# 16.  Spain Again

We sold our house very quickly and flew to Madrid, where we put our boys into a Spanish school and lived with my parents-in-law until Carlos found a job. It was the early eighties and the unemployment in Spain was high, so Carlos bought a second-hand car and travelled the Iberian Peninsula up and down, job hunting, while I stayed behind in Madrid so that the boys could stay in school. The poor mites couldn't speak Spanish at all so it was quite a jolt for them. In fact, I couldn't speak Spanish either, but kids pick up languages far quicker than adults and while the boys were speaking it within a couple of weeks, it took me almost twelve years to speak Spanish, probably because I found it so hard to adapt to the Spanish way of life and put up a mental block all around me. Our friends were amazed because Carlos and I had had the two children and still couldn't speak each other's languages for years, until gradually we both started speaking a mixture of English and Spanish, or *Spanglish* as it is called.

After Carlos had run around Spain looking for a job, but to no avail, we decided that when the boys were on long summer holidays, we would go to the Canary Islands, because we had been told that there would be more opportunities there and, being a tourist destination, I would probably find a job too. So on the first day of the kid's holiday we set off in our second-hand jalopy, with everything we owned and head for the coastal town of Cadiz. We took a ferry from Cadiz to Tenerife where we stayed in a cheap, but lovely hotel. Carlos and I would take turns going out every day job hunting, while the boys spent their time at the pool with either Carlos or I, depending who was to stay at the hotel. The kids had a whale of a time, but Carlos and I were worried because there weren't any jobs on the Island either. After a month we packed up and left Tenerife, with the idea of going back to Madrid. At least we had a roof over our heads there in Carlo's parent's house and the kids could continue school after the long three-month holiday.

On our drive back from Cadiz we passed the straits of Gibraltar and it was a beautiful day and we were won over. We decided to spend the night in Algeciras before continuing on our way the next day. The following morning, on seeing the boys still asleep and obviously exhausted, Carlos decided to have a look around Algeciras to see what the job market was like, so we decided to stay another day. That night he came back to the hotel with a job. And so we stayed. We found a flat to rent and schools for the boys. It was a relief to have a salary coming in because we were getting short. We had left all our money in South Africa because it was difficult to take out at that time. We left it with a friend who was manager of a bank and he told us that when we were ready he would do the transactions for us and send us the money.

Ivan adapted to school and continued the karate lessons he had started in South Africa and Xavier began at a pre-school and went to art lessons in the afternoon. They were both speaking Spanish now and seemed to adapt quite well to Spanish life. Carlos was relatively happy at work but the dingy flat we were in was getting to him. We didn't want to change flats because this one was very convenient for schools and work, all within walking distance. We started talking about getting a house and so we got our capital out of South Africa and started house-hunting.

After about three years, we bought a plot of land with lovely views of the straits and Gibraltar. We designed our own house and had it built by local builders. We moved in, got a dog and Carlos started working for himself. We seemed to have it all but I wasn't happy and it wasn't long before we decided to emigrate to Australia. Carlos applied for a job and was summoned to the Australian consulate in Madrid, eight hours drive away from where we lived, for an interview, because there was someone out from Australia doing interviews at the time. He was told that they needed people like him in Australia and that he should go home, sell his house and wait for the necessary documents, which would be sent to him. Along with these documents, we would have to have all the medical check-ups. Before the interview we had filled in forms, given references, got police clearances from all the countries we had lived in and we also had all the necessary points for age and language, etc.

We sold our house, gave up the business and took the kids out of school and then the big brown envelope arrived. We whooped with joy and then opened it. Inside was a letter saying that we weren't suitable for Australia. Our world turned upside down. So off we went to Madrid and asked them to explain their change of heart but all they said was, "We don't have to give any explanations".

We felt like criminals and now we had no home. Carlos and I are so good we are boring. We don't even drink coffee, so what had happened between the interview and now, we had no idea. We decided then to go to Australia for a holiday and to look around, but the consulate told us that once you have been refused entry to live in Australia, they put you on the blacklist for five years and you can't even go for a holiday. It was clear that we were up against Spanish bureaucracy, something that didn't have anything to do with the nice Australian who had interviewed Carlos but who had gone back to Australia, so we couldn't ask him what had gone wrong, although Carlos has held it against the Australian authorities ever since. Having given up everything that was our lives until then, we had nothing to lose, so after making enquiries from the New Zealand consulate, we decided to go to New Zealand instead. Their consulate said that we would have no problem emigrating there at all.

The day we had put our house on the market, a gypsy family came to see it and bought it straight away. They paid us with wads of notes which they took out of a smelly fish bag. They weren't dealing with banks, but that wasn't our problem.

We went to Auckland and then to Christchurch, where Carlos got a job. The boys were put into schools and I planned to get a job once the boys had adapted to their new schools, but things weren't that good. Firstly, the salaries were not as good as in Spain, which surprised us. And then, there was no national health service. We had started looking around to buy a house, so that when our permanent residence permits came through we could settle down. But Carlos and I were unsure as to whether we had made the right move. New Zealand is a lovely country with lovely people, but financially we were going to be worse off and then Carlos started doing calculations and thinking about his future pension and all in all it didn't seem a viable option to stay. We were all very sorry to leave but we also considered our aging family members back in Europe and really thought it wise to go back to Spain.

So we came back to Spain again and settled down in the little rural town of Los Barrios, the boys started school once more and Carlos got a job, while I did the housework like a good Spanish mama. We stayed in this little village for twelve years and were very happy there, until my health started giving me problems and the house and garden got too much for me, so we sold up and moved closer to Gibraltar, where Carlos was working, about fifteen minutes from where we were living before.

We got a small flat that I could manage to maintain with ease. I had been diagnosed with fibromyalgia and thyroid problems, so a smaller place was easier for me. Due to my condition, I also gave up driving, but where we live now is within walking distance from everything and everywhere, which is very handy. We live in La Linea de la Concepcion, which is right in front of the Rock of Gibraltar and I can walk across, show my passport, and go over for a good strong cup of English tea whenever the mood takes me.

# 17.  Reflections

I always wanted to live in a little cottage, in a country town, somewhere pretty, in England. But my fate took me along other paths. Parents put their children in situations that they think is the right way and children don't really have a say in the matter. If I had had a say in my fate, I think I would have loved to stay put in one place and to grow up knowing my neighbours and having friends for life. When I think back to my childhood in Africa, it seems to be a distant dream and sometimes I wonder whether it happened at all, but it did and it changed me. I lived the life of a little white picaninny, totally free and wild, until the age of six, when all that freedom came to an end and I had to go to boarding school. I have read numerous books on African childhoods, mostly about the modern Africa and although I recognise the scenario, I feel I was lucky to have lived there when there was no TV, videos, computers, electricity and at times no running water. There were also no tourists to spoil the silence.

I was a lonely child and because of it I am now a lonely adult, by choice I admit, because I became accustomed to the silence of the bush as a child and now, still find that I prefer solitude. I see films about Africa and think "that isn't *my* Africa". And yet, deep down, I know that it never was, nor will be, my Africa. But at the time, sitting on the banks of an African river at dawn, totally naked, totally alone and only with the sounds of the bush around me, it was my Africa.

As I have said, I now live in Spain and have found it hard to adapt, probably because Africa runs in my veins and will stay deep within me until the day I die. There is a saying in Maun, that if you drink the waters of the river Thamalakane, you will return, but I guess it will be my ashes that go back there one day to be scattered on the muddy waters to the sound of the fish eagle as it flies above.

I have a problem with colonialism and even as a child I felt that something about the whole system wasn't right, but a child has difficulty comprehending such adult issues. I know my father was doing what he thought was right at the time and I know that he was bought up himself with the colonial attitude being "normal". I sometimes feel that maybe we shouldn't interfere in things that don't belong to us, to change whole nations to suit our way of thinking, educating, living, worshipping. I am not a politician, nor do I dare to assume that I am an especially intelligent person, but although we may have taken some good to these foreign lands, in education and health issues, I sometimes wonder whether we haven't turned the people of these countries into victims. And this we see in so many countries that we have colonised in the past.

Alcohol, drugs, unemployment, loss of local customs and religious beliefs, total displacement in some cases and all to our benefit. We have hunted until all has been hunted, we've over constructed, altered the courses of rivers to suit our farms, we've employed (some think the better word would be enslaved) the locals to look after our children and clean our houses and work our land, land that we have taken over from the very folk that are now our servants, we dress them as we would like to see them dressed, we educate them as we would see fit, just enough, not too much, because then they become "too white". We coax them to our churches, threatening them with hellfire and brimstone. We pride ourselves by saying that we are helping them, educating them, saving them from hell, when they have their own beliefs that are just as valid as ours. We say that we are feeding and clothing them. Yes, we did feed them, with dog/boys meat (the toughest cuts). We did clothe them, with madam's or master's old clothes and scuffed shoes. We gave them a roof over their heads. Yes we did that too, we gave them the servants quarters at the bottom of the yard, scorching in summer, freezing in winter and if they were lucky, they had a drop loo and a cold shower. And yes, we paid them a wage and what a wage it was too. Probably the worst thing we gave these people was the desire to want the things we had, all these things that have made our western world the place it is today, the place we all now strive to leave. We go to Africa for holidays today, to escape our Western World, to find peace and try to 'find ourselves'. Ironic, it surely is. And when we gave them independence, we simply left, walked away and left them to it, without another thought. Now, I am nobody to judge whether we made victims of nations but as a child of colonialism, I have an opinion about the children of white colonialists.

I have sometimes in the past thought that I was a victim, that all children who went through what I did, were victims. Now don't get me wrong, I am not bemoaning my past, just analysing it. My father said that he had no choice but to send me to boarding school because we lived in the bush. A lot of British parents joined the colonial service for adventure because they were bored with the English way of life. I just feel that these things should be thought through with care if you have children. I was cared for by servants more than by my mother, as were most white children. Not because she was out at work but because she had servants to do everything for her. Boarding school broke me as far as I was concerned, especially when you had to accept that your parent's social life came first and you were left alone at school because of it. Bush stations were lonely places too and I had no friends at most times of my childhood. I do, however, want to say that I appreciated the Africa that I came to know and the people of Botswana with whom I came into contact and shared my life. I give thanks for what the experience gave me in the long run, although if given the choice to do it all over again, would I? I really don't know.

~ End ~

# *Epilogue*

Since leaving Botswana after Independence Day on 30th of September, 1966 I have travelled widely and lived fully. Some things about that era I have tried to forget, other things I have tried to maintain in my mind. There is a saying that once you have drunk the waters of Africa, Africa will be forever within you, and you will return. I have returned many times and now realise that Africa is not mine and never was, but I am grateful for what Africa has given me and for the part of it I carry within me forever.

Through the actions of my parents, I became part of the colonial system without having any say in the matter. I cannot say for sure whether my life would have been better or worse had I not lived through that experience but I am grateful for having lived in Botswana at that particular time. It will always live within me and I hope that by sharing these anecdotes with you, it will leave a little bit of Africa within you too.

**Sue Read-Lobo**
Spain, 2011